My Mother's Purse

Edited by

Rosanna McGlone

Editor & Publisher Rosanna McGlone

Writers Pat Grubb, Barbara Tozer, Mary Jean Sinclair, Pam Smith, Pat Sieling, Mike Reeves and Jackie Kirk

Cover photograph Mike Reeves

Printers ImprintDigital.com, Exeter

If you would like to work with Rosanna on a project of your own or buy a copy of this book please contact us at 2 Ancaster Avenue, Lincoln, Lincolnshire, LN2 4AY or email mcglonehealey@yahoo.com

First edition

ISBN 978-1-7399556-1-8

To my mother, Rosie McGlone, with all my love

Table of Contents

Foreword

What do you do when a bomb lands in your bedroom or you're challenged by a German border guard? How do you build a successful career like Mike when people doubt you can? What really goes on behind a Gang Show? And is 'The Good Life' really all it's cracked up to be? These are just some of the questions you'll find answered in this book.

My Mother's Purse is the result of a lot of hard work by a lot of people. Supported by the Care Plus Group Charitable Trust, this memory writing project began in the depths of the pandemic, providing both writing skills and a sense of community for its elderly participants across North East Lincolnshire. It went ahead amid hip replacements and, almost, required sessions directly from hospital beds.

Whilst the participants are currently based in the county in which most of their stories are set, they have come from locations as varied as Dunstable and the Welsh valleys and their narratives even extend as far as Germany before the fall of the Berlin Wall.

The average age of participants was eighty and one of our writers is eighty-nine.

The first part of the project took place on Zoom over five months and was a mixture of workshops and one-to-one mentoring sessions, culminating in this anthology. The second part is yet to come and will be an opportunity for these stories to be shared within the wider community. If you work in a school, or other community setting, and would like to hear the stories from one of the writers themselves, please do contact us.

Why *My Mother's Purse*? Certain memories remain in our heads. I vividly recall, as a child of six, being sent to the corner shop to buy a loaf of Mother's Pride. At the till I opened my mother's purse to take out the coins, and was horrified to see my tiny, baby teeth grinning back at me. At that moment I realized that there was no such thing as the tooth fairy. Our memories are full of stories and revelations, things we wished we'd known, incidents we wish had stayed hidden. This anthology explores our past with an endearing mixture of humour and pathos.

It has been my privilege to support such a fascinating group of people in sharing their memories. What they have learnt from me, is nothing compared to what I have learnt from them. I hope that you will enjoy their stories as much as I have.

Rosanna McGlone

Pat Grubb

Pat Grubb **Where I'm From**

I come from sharing.
Small house, large family. Never quite enough to go round.
Sharing shoes, books, beds and bicycles; clothes, combs and closeness.
Sharing genes with ancestors unknown; a never-met grandmother who painted.
I too paint, sharing ideas with my granddaughter; she also paints,
Following a great-great-grandmother that she never knew.
Wish we had.

I come from learning.
Chewed pencils, ink-smeared fingers, screwed-up eyes
trying to read the blackboard.
Homework hastily completed on the bus to school.
Eleven-plus, grammar school, more homework, leading to various 'Levels'.
Half a lifetime later, college assignments, university, then
Hooray! A teaching degree. Learning how to teach children to learn.
A great job.

I come from making
Ends meet, decisions, mistakes, plans, my mind up, something from nothing.
Making do, making a go of it, making merry, making money, making promises.
Cutting, stitching, gluing, stuffing, knitting, sewing, painting.
Modelling, moulding, mashing, mixing, mending.
Making friends, a family, a home, we've made it!
A busy life.

I come from growing.
Hands deep in the yeasty soil, coaxing out flowers and fruit,
Violas and vegetables, carrots and cabbages, lilacs and leeks.
Growing chickens, children, networks, a history, a family tree.
Growing knowledge, skills, insight, ingenuity, patience.
Growing more stout, more wise, more cynical, more shrewd,
more tactless.
Growing old.

I come from leaving.
Abandonment, departing, renouncing.
My mother left her family and her damp green Irish home to
meet my father,
Who left us, to go who knows where or why?
My once-close family all left to their own devices, left behind.
Friends, some left by their own wish, others would have stayed
If death hadn't beckoned them so fiercely.
Too many gone.

Beginnings

'Oh! My poor head! Will you children ever stop fighting! Patsy, stop being so greedy and share with your brothers!' I sighed. This was a familiar cry in our house. I loved all the scraps around meal preparation, such as bacon rinds, like deliciously greasy, crispy, chewing gum. A couple of strings of it could be chomped for ages. I loved nutty-tasting, slightly chewy cheese rinds too. In fact, I loved all kinds of food, and never seemed to get enough. I sighed again and looked at my brothers – David, wiry and dark haired, five years old; Nigel, stocky, fair and freckled, two years younger; and chubby Timothy. He didn't count really; he was just a baby and couldn't even walk properly yet, let alone talk.

We were hanging around the kitchen, hoping that it would soon be teatime. My mother clearly wanted us out from under her feet. 'Come on, you two, we'll eat it outside!' At seven, I was the oldest and I liked to boss the little ones around. We trooped out to the garden and sat on the back doorstep as I broke the bacon rinds and shared them round.

We lived on a long street with two symmetrical arcs opposite each other like a knot in a ribbon. Our house was on the corner of the left-hand close, so we had a larger front garden than the other houses, but a smaller back one. I don't remember the back much, only that it was triangular, containing a washing line and a huge white lilac tree. The latest baby was always put under that lilac tree to sleep in the big Silver Cross pram until they were old enough to crawl around.

The large front garden, however, could be anywhere: it was the jungle, full of marauding beasts; it was the pitiless desert with miles to go before the oasis; it was a forest where all manner of sprites and elves might be lurking. In other words, that expanse of unkempt, overgrown straggly grass and weeds was whatever our fertile imaginations wanted it to be.

As we sat there, chewing our bacon rinds, Mrs Turpin, our next-door neighbour, came round to speak to our mother.

'Quick, run; it's the witch!' I whispered. We scurried round the corner to avoid her – we were a bit scared of her as she seemed very old, and was always grumpy, frequently shouting at any children around to: 'Go away and play somewhere else, you little pests!'

'Have you seen my cat anywhere, Jean? I'm so worried, it's not like him to go off; he hasn't even been for his food.' She sounded really upset. I decided this was my chance to get in her good books.

'Come on, boys, let's find her cat! Then she will have to be nice to us!' I led my brothers down the street, peering under hedges and making kissy noises in gateways. We arrived at the waste ground at the bottom of the street and started thrashing our way through the long grass.

'Look! Here it is!' shouted Nigel triumphantly, pointing at an object near his feet.

'I don't think she'll want it back like that,' muttered David doubtfully. I overruled him, from my lofty big sister eminence, declaring that she would be able to have a funeral instead of eternal wondering and worrying, ‘You wait and see – she’ll be really pleased with us. She might even give us money for sweeties.’

So we dragged the stiffened, stinking carcass to Mrs Turpin’s front step, knocked on the door and stood with smiling, innocent faces, waiting for praise, congratulations and maybe even a reward. She was horrified and furious, sending us off with a flea in our ears.

At last, it was teatime. ‘Patsy, I need you to go to the shop for me!’ called my mum.

‘Do I have to?’ I moaned, resentful that the boys were allowed to carry on playing, while I had the onerous task of fetching bread for our tea. I walked down the street and crossed the main road to the shops. I knew I had to stop at the kerb, looking and listening carefully before crossing. Of course, traffic was much scarcer in those days, but even at only six or seven years old, I felt quite safe and grown up, especially as I was carrying My Mother’s Purse. It was a hot day and the row of shops seemed a long way off. My legs ached and I had a persistent fly buzzing round my sweaty head.

‘Well, that’s a cross little face,’ smiled Peggy in the baker’s shop. It was always a treat to see her. She had a pretty face and long blonde hair braided into plaits coiled around her ears. She could usually find a broken biscuit to bring a smile to a grumpy child’s face.

‘My mummy said to get a large white bloomer, please, Peggy.’ After I had handed over the cash and tucked The Purse carefully in the waistband of my shorts, Peggy passed down the white tissue-paper-wrapped loaf to me. I took it in my arms, feeling as if I was carrying a baby, a warm, aromatic, golden-skinned bundle. As I walked homewards, I could feel its slightly yielding weight banging on the top of my thighs with each step. The top end of the loaf was just under my nose, tantalising me with its warm yeasty perfume. A flake of the golden crust scratched my chin, so I absentmindedly nibbled it off. Chewing thoughtfully, I glanced down, to notice a hole where I had bitten the bread. Oh dear, I thought, I'd better try and even it up. So, I nibbled a tiny bit more.

And so it continued. By the time I had bitten through the crust completely to reveal the luscious, chewy, crumbly interior, I was lost. I couldn't stop nibbling, biting, chewing. When I reached our house, the top of the 'baby's head' was gone and I was very apprehensive as to the maternal reaction to this mishap. After all, it wasn't really my fault – was it? Before I turned into the garden path, I carefully manoeuvred the loaf until the desecrated end was downward facing. But it wasn't many minutes before my crime was discovered and I was in big trouble. 'You are such a greedy little girl,' said my mother resignedly.

School Days

I ran happily into the school playground towards my beloved friend, Dilly, but when I spotted who she was talking to, my heart faltered. My steps slowed as I glanced from side to side, frantically trying to find a way to escape, but I was hemmed in on all sides. Slowly, unwillingly, pressed on by the small bodies all around me, I drew nearer until, shy and bashful, I was looking up at her. 'Whatever's up with you, sprog? You look scared to death,' teased Janice, Dilly's cousin; the older, wiser, sophisticated cousin, who always seemed to be laughing at my tongue-tied embarrassment.

My earliest school days were spent in Mrs Gilmour's front parlour. She was a well-meaning neighbour who ran a 'Sunday School', trying, I suppose, to instil virtue into the little heathens who had taken over her genteel part of Hertfordshire. I didn't like it much, as it was, quite frankly, a bit boring. But that was only on a Sunday afternoon. The next step along the education path took me to a nursery school, where we were forced to nap every afternoon on folding canvas camp beds. I hated it, because my bed was at the end, where one of the teachers chose to sit to drink her after-lunch cuppa, squashing my feet in the process.

But it was such bliss when at last I attended proper school, the local primary. I loved every minute of it. I loved all the books, I loved the games, I loved my teacher, Miss Stephenson, and I loved my new friend Dilly. I adored her the moment she came to stand calmly by my side on our first day, as if she had chosen me. I liked the self-possessed way she held herself, her little tucked-in smile, and her long straight hair, woven into neat pigtails. I was scatter-brained, wayward, disorganised, my socks always falling down and my wild curly hair always losing its hair ribbons. Dilly was how I wanted to be. We spent every day together, lessons and playtimes. My life with Dilly in it was marvellous. Until the cousin showed up, walking with Dilly to and from school. She must have been at least nine years old, and just as I adored Dilly, so Dilly adored Janice.

'Hiya, Dils. Come on, walk in with me,' Janice would call. Dilly would run delightedly towards her, gesturing to me to follow. But I wasn't having any of it. Consumed with jealousy, I would slouch and sulk; this rival for my friend's affections was too grown up for me to cope with. Of course, Janice didn't realise any of this; to her, I was just the weird, scruffy little girl that was always hanging round with Dilly.

'Come here, sprog, I've got something to tell you,' Janice called to me this particular morning. As I sidled grudgingly towards her, she said, 'Guess what! You're coming home with me 'n' Dilly after school today. Your mum said you can come for tea, then sleep over.' I gaped up at her disbelievingly. I hardly ever went home with other children, and I had certainly never stayed at someone else's house.

'It's true,' giggled Dilly. 'My mum spoke to your mum, and it's all arranged. Are you pleased?' I nodded so vigorously that my hair ribbon slipped off, leaving my hair a curly mess over my face. Today was surely the best day of my life. Not only were we walking down the hill to have lessons in the church hall later today, which was a treat in itself, but at the end of school I would be turning up the hill to unknown territory, to Dilly's house.

Dilly and I rushed breathlessly into school, laughing and giddy. We could hardly concentrate. Miss Stephenson had to keep reprimanding us, saying, 'Whatever's the matter with you two today? Please pay attention.'

We were reprieved when we walked to the church hall. We paired up for the crocodile and walked together, swinging our hands and chattering our plans for the evening. 'I'll get all my dollies out and we can play schools – or – no, do you want to play skipping outside?' I wasn't really listening; I was trying to work out the phrase 'all my dollies'. How many did she have? Surely no one had more than one doll? My mummy always said one was enough, and I had to share that one with my brothers. Luckily, they never really wanted to play with her; I was always worried they would be too rough.

At the church hall, we had to sit in different groups, so there was no more chance for whispered plans. I liked the church hall; the booming of our feet on the wooden boards; the birds swooping over our heads, nesting in the open rafters; the musty, dusty smell. It must have been a nightmare for the teachers. I usually got into trouble because I would be reading a book under cover of my desk, a book totally unconnected to the lesson. I would be so engrossed that I never noticed when Mrs Burt walked around the room, reaching over my shoulder to snatch the book from my grasp.

Finally, the afternoon was over. We could go home and I was going home with Dilly. I even thought that I might begin to like Janice. After all, it was her who had announced the wonderful plan for the evening.

I found Dilly's home strange. It was so very tidy, and so quiet.

Her mum greeted her with: 'Hello, you, have you had a lovely day?', followed by a stroke of the hair, a drink of milk, and shop-bought biscuits. It was even better when I had a stroke of the hair too, except I was a bit concerned that my hair wouldn't feel smooth like Dilly's. Then the house was silent, apart from Dilly and I speaking to each other and the dollies. At my house, the wireless was always on, the boys would be bickering with each other, and the baby was usually crying. My harassed mother was too busy for more than, 'Hello, just go and rock the pram for me, will you?'

I was very conscious of my manners at teatime; I knew I mustn't let my family down. Dilly had so many dolls of all different kinds. She let me play with the one I liked the best, a small Rosebud doll with a full set of beautifully hand-made clothes. But it was quite a relief when it was decided we'd played long enough, and it was time for bed. In my camp bed in Dilly's room, I could relax, clutching 'Rosie'.

When Dilly's mum came into the bedroom to kiss her goodnight, I kept my eyes tight shut, pretending to be asleep so I didn't get into trouble. I heard her mother say, 'Dilly, why don't you let her keep Rosie? After all, you've got so many dolls. You can spare one, I'm sure.'

This was in 1951; we were both five years old. It's been seventy years since I last saw Dilly. My family moved away shortly afterwards, and I never saw her again. But I have a photograph of an old-fashioned little girl, with long pigtails and a secretive smile. I have memories of the first and purest love of my young life, and I still have that little doll, complete with its full set of hand-made clothes.

A Special Person

All is quiet. My three little brothers are asleep upstairs; the only sounds are the gentle crackle of the fire, the clicking of my mother's needles and the whisper of my turning pages. I am seven years old, beginning to enjoy reading to myself; my book is all bright colours and few words on each page. My mother is enjoying a moment's quiet in the glow of the fire. We feel no need to speak, we are at peace in each other's company.

Suddenly the silence is cracked by the crash of the door flinging open. A tall, lean, dark shape is in the room. With two strides he is at my mother's side; an arm raised and lowered sharply, once, twice, three times. With muttered angry words, he lurches back through the door, banging it closed behind him, leaving us to a different silence this time it is broken only by my mother's sobs and my frightened, panting whimpers.

That evening in 1952 is my last and only memory of my birth father. He left us that night, to live our lives in happy, heedless penury, untroubled by the ways of any male figure over the age of five. Until Bert came into our lives.

Bert came to all the houses on our road in his role of seller of insurance policies, vacuum cleaners, and new-fangled knitting machines. He had the charm of a born salesman and all the housewives enjoyed his friendly banter when he came to collect their weekly insurance premiums or to demonstrate one of his machines. I don't think he sold many vacuum cleaners, and even fewer knitting machines. Any he did sell would have been on the 'never-never', the easy payment plan of the day, so he had those payments to collect also.

As children, we didn't pay him much heed until he started staying a little longer at our house, taking a cup of tea and a slice of cake before he continued his rounds. He would often bring us sweets or comics and would hoover our threadbare carpets with us children sitting on the cylinder shrieking and giggling with excitement.

I think my mother fell in love with his kindness, his dark good looks, and his affection for her children. Maybe he fell in love with her fruit cake. Anyway, they got together and to escape wagging tongues – it was quite scandalous in those days to be a divorced woman – we moved to the other side of the county. Life was much happier there.

The boys accepted this man as their father quickly, but I was warier. I must have been difficult to deal with, a prickly, defensive, untrusting little girl, full of cheek and arguments. 'Do I have to?' or 'Why should I?' was my frequent cry. He never lost his temper with me, and he never got cross with the boys.

My brother told me about the time my mother told Bert to take the stick to him, the one she kept by the back door. He says he must have done something really bad but can't remember what. In order to keep what little peace there was in those days, Bert dutifully took the dreaded stick down from its place, took my brother outside to where Mum couldn't see and told him to bend over. My brother braced himself for what was to come, but was relieved and surprised to see, through his legs, Bert acting out the prescribed 'six of the best', by hitting the wall, and not his backside. In spite of having this brood of four unruly hooligans to care for, when our new baby sister came along, he was as kind and caring as ever.

I remember him in soft, worn checked shirts with his sleeves rolled up, always fixing something, working steadily with his pipe clenched between his teeth. For instance, when the Bakelite knob on a saucepan lid broke off, he spent hours with a scrap of firewood, whittling and carving with his penknife until he had a workable replacement to screw onto the lid.

He loved to argue politics (he was a staunch member of a trades union). His beliefs were simple: that religion was the opium of the masses; that everyone you met had a worthwhile story to tell; that if each person took only what they needed and contributed everything they were able, the world would work just fine. He had been in the Marines during the Second World War and kept his medals in a scratched Oxo tin. When the boys pestered him for stories about the war, he merely laughed softly, saying, 'Well, it was plain boring most of the time. Lots of sitting around. Lots of cleaning stuff.'

He loved reading his newspaper and muttering about the idiocies of whichever government was in power. He spent his weekends gardening to provide my mother with the flowers she loved and vegetables to put on the table. Most Sundays, he would drive us in his sage green Ford Thames van to the countryside for a picnic, not even hearing the squabbling going on in the back until my mother would cry in exasperation, 'Stop that right now, or we're turning straight back home again!'

Then he would mutter in his calm voice, more to pacify her than quieten us, 'Now then, you lot, calm down! We're nearly there now.'

The following narrative describes the kind of man Bert was. He had decided it would be a great idea to take us all on holiday to Woolacombe in Devon. He bought an army surplus bell tent, heavy brown canvas with a tall wooden pole holding up the central peak. This tent, a small Calor gas cooking stove, bedding from our beds, boxes and bags holding shoes, clothes, nappies, cans of food, bottles, the baby's potty, toys, saucepans, books and more, was duly loaded into the gallant Ford Thames.

With us four older kids laid across the top of the heap and the baby on Mother's knee, we set off. We had packets of Spangles to swap and share to make the journey go by without too much squabbling, so all went well until we reached the notorious Porlock Hill, a vertiginous road which curved away at the top out of sight. The poor van, unable to cope with its unnatural burden, stalled on the first slopes like an unwilling nag, and began to roll backwards. My mother started screaming, until Bert pulled in at the side of the road, saying calmly, 'It's OK, we'll just have to take a bit of the weight out.'

Did I mention it was raining? We clambered from the van, each bringing something with us, until we had a pile of possessions growing steadily in height and dampness on the verge. The rain dripped down from the trees onto our miserable heads as we huddled at the side of the road. As a bright red sports car swished past us up the hill, trying to get up enough speed to avoid stalling, just as we had, we were sprayed with muddy water from the deluge running in the gutter. Dripping like a cat hauled from a water butt, clutching the sodden baby, my mother hurled invectives at the receding car. It was the first time I had ever heard her swear. Bert stood, hands on hips, surveying the saturated family before him.

'Now then, don't fuss,' he said calmly, 'it's only a bit of water. It'll all be fine.'

The rain did ease off. We were rescued by a troop of boy scouts who cheerfully carried our stuff and pushed the van to the top of the hill. We eventually arrived at our campsite, and Bert was right, it did all turn out fine. It was a great holiday.

Bert, my dad, taught me patience, fortitude, tolerance and kindness to others; he showed me how to make the best of what I had, and not to compare myself to others. He had another three children with my mother, bringing our family to eight children, and he treated us all with the exact same amount of affection and care. My father may have disappeared from my life, but the man who took his place was far better, he was a true dad.

The Good Life?

Time has a habit of passing; life always moves on. My five brothers, two sisters and I all eventually grew up and went away. Like a blown dandelion clock, we all drifted to different places; the furthest away was a sister who ended up in Southern France. Most of the other siblings landed in places in the South of England. As for me, I wafted around Britain, from Scotland, to Wiltshire, to Norfolk, and finally found myself rooted in Lincolnshire, having gathered to myself a husband and two children along the way.

Arriving in this small village, Marshchapel, near the coast in the north of the county, felt like coming home. But a home like I had never known before. I had always lived in towns, or large housing estates on the outskirts of towns, where neighbours were friendly enough but everyone had their own lives to live. Here, it seemed people wanted to share their life with you and expected you to share yours with them.

We moved into our bungalow in December 1973, in a snowstorm. Our home was the first one occupied in this cul-de-sac of little houses, built in what had once been a large garden and orchard, the first of many such developments in the village. My son was six years old, and my daughter a baby of six months. We had barely unpacked the essentials when the power cut hit. This was fairly problematic as the modern bungalow was all electric, including heating.

There soon came a knock at the door – outside was a friendly, genial figure. 'Now then, I reckon you folks'll be feeling the cold,' the visitor said in a broad Lincolnshire dialect. 'I live just by there, and saw you move in, saw the young 'uns, thought you might be needin' this.' He hauled in a large oil heater, which judging by its weight, was well filled with fuel. This Good Samaritan, Jim, was our nearest neighbour, the proprietor of the village shop and post office round the corner. He proved to be a dear and wonderful friend for many years. As did the next caller, who brought a camping lamp, and the one after that, Kath, who offered to, 'Warm milk for the baby, or make you some food if you want. I've got an Aga cooker.'

These people were all strangers to us; they were 'nosy neighbours' who had watched our arrival with interest and were all concerned with our welfare. This set the tenor of our lives for many years. We only moved once more, and that move was to a bigger house just round the corner. We were totally accepted and enfolded into village life.

Both my children attended the village school, and eventually, I too went to it, as the school cook. I loved that job. I was my own boss. I could do what I wanted; go home to put my washing out, take in a parcel; as long as the lunch was edible and on the table by twelve noon on the dot, the headmaster gave me total autonomy. I pride myself that the children all enjoyed my meals and hardly anyone brought a packed lunch. There was a manual that laid down which particular food groups should be dished up each month. For instance, chicken twice a month, fish every week, beef mince twice a month, and TVP (textured vegetable protein) every week. It was up to each individual cook to decide on how these items were served. One example; to use the allocation of dried milk, flour and eggs, I would make milkshake with doughnuts or Chelsea buns, a much more popular choice than rice pudding.

To help me in the kitchen, I had two determined ladies who had worked there 'since Adam was a boy'. Shirley, lean and wiry, with a great puff of nicotine-yellowed hair falling from her cook's cap, was the veg-prep lady, and she kept me up to date with all the village news, dalliances, and scandal, related in a gravelly smoker's voice. I think she enjoyed having a brand-new audience to listen to and be awed by her tales of past and present.

Stout Geraldine, in charge of washing-up, was more taciturn. She spoke mainly in gruff monosyllables, either to contradict Shirley or to complain about me and my 'new-fangled cooking ideas'. She was of the 'give 'em stodge and stand over them while they eat it' school of catering. If I gave the children what she considered to be 'ower fancy food' like, maybe, gravy AND apple sauce with pork, she would demonstrate her displeasure with a loud, tuneless, continuous warbling hum. I was quite pleased when she retired.

Since we had moved to the more spacious house, with a much bigger garden, we thought we would give 'The Good Life' a go. So I visited a farmer friend, Marjie, for advice on keeping chickens.

'What's the matter with that one?' I asked her, as we leant on the gate, watching her hens scratching around in their run. The one I was looking at was crouching alone, hunched and miserable, almost totally bald, under a clump of nettles.

'It's right at the bottom of the pecking order; none of the others will tolerate it at all. I'm afraid it will have to go, if only to put it out of its misery,' she replied briskly. I agreed, trying not to flinch at her unfeeling common sense. There are some aspects of life on which a vegetarian and a farmer will never see eye-to-eye, and these things are best skirted around for the sake of friendship. But while we sat drinking our afternoon tea, I couldn't stop thinking of that poor creature having to die for the crime of being unpopular.

'OK,' I said, suddenly decided, 'I'll have it!' Marjie, when she understood what it was I wanted to have, tried to talk some sense into me. I didn't have a hen-run or a house for it; I knew nothing about hens or how to look after them; my husband would do his nut; it would ruin my garden, and so on. But the more she argued, the more wonderful seemed my idea. I would save this one creature's life, it would become sleek and plump, and would become my loving companion as I worked in my garden...

Of course, real life is not like that. My long-suffering husband had built a hen-house, and fenced off a corner of the garden, so 'Baldy' and a couple of other misfits Marjie had thrown in to keep her company took possession of their new home. Armed with a book from the library, *Back-Yard Poultry Keeping*, we were all set for 'The Good Life'.

A week later, I was snivelling sadly over the stiff lifeless body of my best hen, the only one without a physical deformity, the pride of my flock. (I know 'flock' is a bit grand for three birds, but I feel it's important to use the correct terminology.) Apparently, hens do that, they can just die for no apparent reason, leaving the rest of us to soldier on. This maybe sounds a bit melodramatic to those of you not of the poultry world, but that first death hit me hard. It brought with it an ethical/moral problem, what to do with the body? Dustbin? Compost bin? Feed it to the dog, or leave it out for any passing fox? None of these solutions were quite fitting. At last I hit on the solution. I held a brief but heartfelt funeral, laying dear Betty gently to rest in the runner-bean trench with a nice deep mulch of vegetable peelings and garden trimmings over her. We had some jolly good beans that summer.

Baldy did grow sleek and plump, but became spiteful and bossy, far from the affectionate pet I had imagined. We acquired two fluffy chicks hatched in the school incubator which grew into a huge stately cockerel, and a pretty grey-and-white hen. We named them Sam 'n' Ella. Next came a pair of handsome Blackrocks who laid lovely brown eggs. These were called Michael and Simon; I have no idea why. That was my flock complete.

My chickens benefitted from the children's leftovers. I would walk home after lunch along the lane to my house calling, 'Chook, chook, chookies!' The chickens would run through the fields surrounding my house where they roamed, their long-legged strides easily keeping up with me. They would have scrambled through the hedge and be waiting greedily for me as I came into the garden with their grub.

Next, we acquired a goat, named Daisy. Our plan was that Daisy would clear our large overgrown garden of weeds, ready for growing vegetables. Daisy's plan was to clamber up the couple of stunted apple trees we had inherited, eating any apples before they had a chance to mature, chomp our few rose bushes down to the ground, and turn her disdainful nose up at the weeds.

When she tired of these activities, she would escape the garden to trot out in search of the charms of the billy goat who lived in Grainthorpe, a mile or two up the road. More than once, I would be wreathed in steam, cooking the lunch, when a phalanx of children would pound on the kitchen door, crying out, 'Mrs Grubb, Mrs Grubb! Your Daisy's out again!' I would drop everything with a clang, fly out of the door, through the playground, and out of the gate, pound up the road, flapping my apron to try and attract the blessed goat's attention. Like the tail of a comet, the children would trail after me, all shouting a shrill Greek chorus, 'Daisy, Daisy! Come back!' Such behaviour would no doubt be frowned on in these more safety conscious, more boring, days.

Needless to say, we got rid of the goat, swapping her for a sack of 'tates' and a few sticks of sprouts. She went to enjoy a more restrained and constrained life with a herd of her fellow creatures down the coast in Sutton-on-Sea.

Daisy's place in the garden was taken by a lovely little herd of Aylsbury ducks, hatched under a lamp in the kitchen, then lovingly watched over by the dog as they grew to adulthood in the garden. How I loved those ducks, messy as they were. I loved their quirky characters, their flicky tails, and their dear little faces. I shouldn't have let myself love them. They had been bought with the sole intention of filling the freezer and ultimately, our stomachs. They grew larger and fatter until the day came when it was decided (not by me) that their end was nigh. My husband didn't think he had the necessary skill to do the job, but a willing slaughterer was found in the White Horse, our local pub.

The day of the dreadful deed arrived all too soon; my eight-year-old daughter and I took ourselves off for a walk to avoid the unpleasantness. We came home an hour or so later to a silent garden, overlaid with an air of doom. None of us could contemplate duck as a meal after that; we gave them all away. So, the whole affair was in vain. We decided that 'The Good Life' was not for us. The only animals we share our home and garden with since the dog died, the cat ran away and a fox got all the chickens, are those creatures responsible for themselves – birds, hedgehogs, foxes, the odd badger. That kind of country life is good enough for me.

Barbara Tozer

Barbara Tozer **Where I'm From**

I am from a home of love and laughter
A mum and dad, of course
A brother and a sister
The perfect combination
How lucky am I.

Sitting by the fire, all hands on deck.
Cutting up old coats
Into neat even strips.
Mother made snip mats
One for each outside door.

The smell of burning filled the air
As the bread fell off the toasting fork,
Quickly rescued from the flames
The black scraped off.
Covered in butter and jam for tea.

Winter nights are here
So much to do
Jigsaws, bagatelle, draughts and more
Whilst dad sits contentedly
Smoking his pipe.

Summer days on the beach
Paddling in the warm streams
Left by the ebbing tide
Collecting cockles to take home
Eaten with bread and butter for tea.

Dad worked on the fish docks
Allowed one free bass of fish each week
From haddock to halibut, plaice and lemon sole in between
No great wealth did we have
Yet we lived like kings.

Beginnings

The brown van came trundling down the street of neat, terraced houses where I lived with my mother, father, brother and sister. Mother was crying and all the neighbours were outside watching. The van had come to collect my brother, who had contracted diphtheria which was a very serious illness. It had come to take him to what was called the fever hospital; very often they never came home. It was very upsetting, and all the neighbours watched as the brown van left the street.

No visitors were allowed the whole time my brother was away, about six weeks. Mother would take my sister and me (I remember being in the pram) to the health office each day where there was a glass-fronted notice board outside and the condition of each patient was recorded. I remember clearly, Mother crying all the way home because the report stated my brother was 'very ill'. This had been the message for several days. Mother was so upset that my father cycled all the way to the isolation hospital, which was about three to four miles away, to speak to someone. The result was that the message hadn't been updated and should have read improving. My brother did recover.

We moved to a three-bedroom semi-detached house in May 1939 just before the outbreak of war that same month. My first six weeks there were spent in bed as I contracted scarlet fever. Mother was the only person allowed in the bedroom. My brother and sister had to stay off school.

My dad suffered from shell shock from the First World War and when there was an air raid he couldn't be in a confined space. But my sister, brother and mother and I sheltered in the cupboard under the stairs; it was quite a tight squeeze. Later, we used next door's shelter, climbing over the fence to their shelter, until we had our own. The neighbours would help each other to dig the holes for the shelters which were quite deep with just a curved tin roof showing above ground. I remember being very frightened during the raids.

The most serious raid was when the personnel bombs, called butterfly bombs because of their appearance, were dropped everywhere. Some exploded on landing, but most didn't, which was the idea as when touched, either by curiosity or accidentally, the bomb could kill or seriously maim a person. These bombs were not dropped anywhere else in the whole country, only on Grimsby, Cleethorpes and nearby villages. Apparently, it was a German experiment.

Cleverly, the British government ordered a complete news blackout of the event. The Germans thought the raid was a failure. It wasn't as it caused many deaths and serious injuries. But as a result, it was never repeated anywhere. Afterwards there were many unexploded bombs all around in the streets, parks and playing fields. Those in the street were encircled by sandbags and guarded by an air raid warden. We carried on as normal playing in the street.

On one occasion after the all-clear had sounded we all went back to go to bed when my brother flew back down the stairs shouting, 'There's a bomb! There's a bomb in my bedroom!'

My dad went to fetch the air raid warden for him to deal with the bomb, but the warden said to him, 'It's your house, Cliff, so it's your responsibility till you bring it to the other side of the gate.'

My poor dad, who still suffered with shell shock, had to retrieve the bomb and carry it downstairs through the house whilst we all stood in a long row, watching. I remember it very well. It was white, about fifteen inches long, pointed at one end with a tail at the other. Luckily it didn't go off.

In the local park there were concerts held each day during the school holidays. These were called holidays at home. I really enjoyed them and went almost every day. I especially enjoyed watching the girls from the dancing school. This resulted in me pestering Mother to allow and pay for me to attend tap-dancing classes, which I did for quite some time.

We also did shows; this meant that we had to have different costumes which our mother had to make. We were told which material an outfit required. I knew we couldn't afford to buy new material each time so, when we had to have a black skirt with coloured bias binding stripes around the hem, my mother used the blackout curtains from my brother's bedroom. All windows had to be blacked out at night and no crack of light could be seen. The air raid warden would do his nightly round shouting, 'Put that light out,' if he could see any light at all. Going back to dancing, we were asked to buy lots of taffeta material in various colours. I thought we couldn't possibly afford that, so I left. Mother never knew this was the reason I left.

We spent many happy hours walking to Cleethorpes to spend

the whole day on the beach making sandcastle pies and decorating them with shells and feathers and paddling in the water. Mother would pack sandwiches the night before. Quite often neighbours and family would join us from our street. On one occasion a neighbour was knitting a swimsuit (called bathing costumes then) for her daughter. This she finished and off we went into the water paddling up to our waist. On the way back the swimsuit was so heavy with water it had stretched down to the girl's feet, and she was virtually naked. We did laugh, although not everyone thought it amusing.

It must have been a very difficult time for my parents, but overall, my memories are happy because our home was full of love and laughter. Mother always said you can always see the funny side of most situations.

School Days

'Mama,' I yelled with delight, 'Doreen Webb has got the measles!' Mother was quite taken aback that I was so pleased at someone's misfortune that I had run all the way home from school to relay the good news.

Doreen Webb was a very pretty girl with blonde hair and blue eyes who had just been transferred to our school along with lots more boys and girls from another school which had closed. The boys in our class certainly noticed how pretty Doreen was. Needless to say, we girls were jealous, however that wasn't the reason I was so elated. Doreen had the star part in our school play, and I was her understudy, so now the part was mine, all mine.

In the play my name was Alexandra Dumas, a French girl studying at an English boarding school. We wore navy gymslips and white blouses. My blouse was of white satin with full sleeves. I felt so special.

For weeks before, every night I would repeat everyone's parts so many times that I think my mother knew all the words too. I was the lead and the play was a great success, enjoyed by the whole school and parents alike.

This occurred in the senior school so, going back to the beginning, to my introduction, aged five I started school, a newly built first co-educational school (boys and girls together) in the area. How lovely, I thought as I surveyed the room, which was furnished with round tables in blue, red, yellow and green with matching chairs. The afternoon was spent sitting cross-legged in the school hall watching and listening to the choir rehearse for the musical festival held each year on Cleethorpes Pier.

During the afternoon several pupils raised their arms, to request to go to the toilet. The stern reply came back: 'No, wait until break.' I too needed the toilet but dare not ask. The inevitable happened to me. The headmistress, seeing the wet patch on the floor, made us all stand in a line and felt all the girls' pants until she found the culprit, me. I was smacked very hard and continuously on my arm until it was very red and scratched but I didn't cry. This was Carr Lane School, later to become Havelock School, now demolished and replaced by a beautiful new building on an adjoining site which is still named Havelock.

From age seven to eleven the war was raging. We never missed school even though we had often spent half the night in the air raid shelter. We trotted off to school with our gas mask in its cardboard box hung over our shoulder with string. Some of our lessons were carried out wearing the masks. It was not pleasant. They smelt strongly of rubber and they were so claustrophobic (a little more uncomfortable than the Covid masks that we are wearing now).

When the siren sounded, we went to a school shelter. These were long brick-built buildings in the playground. Inside were long benches where we continued our lessons including singing our times tables. However, most air raid warnings were at night and often there were false alarms. On a few occasions a single bomb would be dropped from stray German bombers.

One lunchtime my brother, who was an errand boy for the Co-op grocery store, was on his delivery bike riding down Freeman Street when he heard a roaring sound. Looking behind, he saw a German plane at rooftop level. He said it filled the sky like a huge black monster, he never pedalled so fast to get away.

Apparently, having passed the preliminary exam to be able to go to the grammar school (not that I can remember taking it) we were sent off to a college in the centre of Grimsby with a pen, pencil and ruler to take the scholarship. I do not recall any mention of swotting or what to expect for the forthcoming exam whatsoever. However, it was up to the senior school for me as I did not pass. I enjoyed my lessons particularly English and PT, physical training.

I found it very frustrating and still do, that girls were not allowed to study science. Our lesson was nature study instead. The boys learnt woodwork and gardening whilst we were taught needlework, cookery and laundry, since there were no washing machines in those days. How strange that although the boys did gardening, whilst we were busy learning to cook, they never produced any vegetables for us to use. I do not know to this day what they actually produced. They also kept rabbits.

As winter approached the needlework teacher would visit the rabbits to select two matching ones for her fur mittens, which she made for herself. I found it so distressing.

My love of PT rewarded me with a place in the netball team, playing home games and visiting other schools after lessons finished. Apart from one or two changes, the same girls remained in the team for the next three years. Freda was my best friend. We discovered that we shared a birthday, our middle name was Ethel (after our respective mothers), we lived two streets away, at number 162, and best of all we both had a brother call Raymond.

Miss Lane our English teacher was very thorough and fair, making a big impression on me. I remember her words after all these years, seventy-seven years actually: 'Never begin a sentence with And, But or So. Also, remember it is "similar to" and "different from".' At fourteen years of age my school days were over. I had to wait until I was fifteen to be old enough to attend evening classes. This I did, and carried on with my English lessons, passing my GCE in English Language, thank you, Miss Lane.

A Special Person

A double decker bus stopped at the zebra crossing as a small elderly lady with white stick aloft toddled across the road followed by a ginger cat. When halfway across she stopped and with her hand on the bus she steadied herself and rested. The driver poked his head out of the cab window and like a roaring bull delivered some choice words. The lady in question was my mother, in her later years, and upon arriving home she said, 'Do you know, the driver swore at me?' She was shocked she hadn't realised it was the bus until the driver shouted. She had very poor eyesight and jam-jar glasses on her round, rosy-cheeked face. Her hair was still dark and she diligently put it up in curlers each night, but during the day her hair was held in place with a fine net. For morning chores she would wear a full pinafore and after dinner, which she freshly cooked every day, she would change into a frilly apron. Her afternoons would be spent sewing, knitting or mending and on Friday afternoons she would clean the silver cutlery.

Even with her poor eyesight mother would use her sewing machine and often upon our arrival home from school, she would still be trying to thread the needle which she had endeavoured to do all afternoon. As either my sister or I threaded the needle for her at the first attempt Mother would say, 'Such good eyesight.' She was neither cross nor exasperated, she was so patient.

Have you ever seen a fine grandfather clock with its hands covered in flour? You would if it happened to be a Wednesday, baking day. The grandfather clock stood proudly in the corner of the room; there was no glass over the dial. With failing eyesight Mother didn't let this stop her from doing what she had always done. Needing to know the time, she pranced on to the settee and with floured hands swept them over the face of the clock, then down she came and carried on baking meat pies, fruit pies, large and small.

On visiting Mother's, she said one time, 'Here is a meat pie for your supper, my love.' On my next visit I was informed that a small fruit pie had gone missing.

'No, it hasn't gone missing,' I said, 'I had it.'

'I gave you a meat pie,' came the reply.

I said, 'Yes, and it was delicious because it consisted of a pastry base, a meat filling, a pastry lid, an apricot filling and a pastry lid. Steak and apricots, like pork and apple, goes well.' Mystery solved.

As Mother was getting older I took over the washing for her and my brother, who still lived at home. My dad was not around, having died at sixty-eight. Mother wore plus fours (also known as bloomers), not trousers, knickers, with white cotton Aertex pants beneath. It should be remembered that she was from the Victorian era. I would purchase these white pants for her. As I arrived for my Saturday visit Mother was busy telling my sister that I had bought her the wrong pants. I said that they were exactly the same as always. Mother said that they couldn't be the same as the new ones were killing her and cutting into her groin.

I asked her to show me, so she lifted her skirt and my sister and I burst out laughing as she was wearing my brother's white cotton Aertex Y-fronts. Mother soon joined in the laughing. Being virtually blind, Mother was not able to tell the difference between the feel of the Y-fronts and her pants. I used to wear a shocking pink cardigan so my mother could see me as a splodge of bright pink around the room when I was there, similar to how she could see the flames in the fire.

When I was about to leave school, it was my dearest wish to work at the food office. I had often visited there as many people did during and shortly after the war. I noticed that lots of girls worked there, and they seemed a happy crowd. However, I was told in no uncertain terms that I could not be employed there as only grammar-school girls were eligible.

Unbeknown to me, off my mother went on her bike to the centre of town to the food office where she asked for an interview with the chief executive officer. She apparently showed him an example of my handwriting and said that I was a neat and tidy girl and would he bend the rules on this occasion. As Mother would have said, 'lo and behold', he did.

When I started, I was told that I would be obliged to take the Civil Service examination. Luckily, I passed and my dream came true due entirely to my mother. I spent a very happy four years there until food rationing was over and the food office closed.

During my time there I discovered such honesty shown by the general public. Many people kept a pig in their back garden, therefore they were required to forfeit their bacon coupons. They would turn up at the food office to present their ration books for the whole family for their bacon coupons to be cancelled.

My mother made a huge impression on my life. Through her influence I learnt to work hard, be patient, show tolerance and be kind. Best of all, I learnt to laugh and be content with what you have.

The Ups and Downs of Shopping

Who would have thought a seemingly innocent afternoon's shopping could end so dramatically? It was a regular occurrence for my sister and I to visit Mother each Saturday to carry out the week's shopping for her.

'Don't be long, will you,' said Mother, 'and please don't go to Mark's.' Marks being Marks & Spencer's which was in Freeman Street, quite a walk from our local supermarket, Ramsdens, on Cleethorpe Road, to which we were heading. We promised that we would only go to the one shop.

Once each year, however, for my eldest sister's birthday, which was imminent, a family gathering was held, so on this particular occasion a great deal of party food and drink was to be purchased from Ramsdens.

Off we went. After quite some time chatting, laughing and generally having a happy time as always when we were together, the trolley was overflowing with all the produce to be paid for.

My sister Beryl wished to go upstairs to the toy department. Beyond the checkouts was a wide staircase at the foot of which stood a security guard. I approached the guard in anticipation and asked if he would be so kind as to mind our trolley whilst we went upstairs. He replied he would not and pointed to the side of the stairs for us to use the moving trolley belt. This was something quite new in our area. The guard did condescend to place the trolley on the belt for us, so we carefully made our way upstairs as the trolley trundled beside us. We were quite amused by this as we happily scoured the toy department for my sister's requirements.

My sister had taken charge of the trolley as we proceeded to go down the stairs to pay for our goods, preceded by myself. I eventually turned around to see where my sister was, only to find her still at the top with the trolley on the belt indicating that it wouldn't move. I signalled for her to give it a push, which she did. Nothing happened, so I indicated for her to push it harder.

It moved and then suddenly began hurtling down the belt. Seeing this and realising that the trolley was approaching far too quickly, I stuck out my arm thinking I could somehow slow it down. Oh yes, it did slow down as it struck me on the thumb. In fact, it was so dramatically stopped in its tracks it rose high into the air in a vertical fashion and so the missile attack began. Trifles, cakes, tins, packets and bottles zoomed through the air in rapid succession.

There was a sea of faces turned upwards and then the neat queues at the checkouts scattered left and right as the missiles rained down. Sounding like explosions, the bottles smashed onto the tiled floor. Babycham, Cinzano and lemonade swilled all over, tins rolled, packets burst open. It was mayhem. Strangely no voices were heard. Everyone seemed to have been struck dumb.

My sister had disappeared from the top of the stairs as two first aiders, seemingly delighted at the prospect of putting their skills into action, came trotting down to me where I was rooted to the spot halfway down the stairs. I knew my sister would be somewhere amongst the toys laughing her head off, as I was marched off to the medical room, where my not too badly injured thumb was dressed. I was then sent on my way.

At this point as I approached the top of the stairs, I spied a notice which read *'Please turn trolley wheels backwards before placing trolley on the belt'.* As I well knew my sister was not in the habit of reading instructions.

Looking rather shame-faced, we descended to the ground floor, where we were greeted by the manager, who said, 'Would madam like to do her shopping again?' This was amazing and gratefully agreed so we resumed our shopping, still highly amused as well as embarrassed.

Upon arrival home, very late, Mother took a lot of convincing that we had only been to the one shop, that was after we had stopped laughing. However, after relaying the events, interspersed by laughing fits, she realised you couldn't make that story up, could you?

The moving trolley belt was never in operation again, and a week later an acquaintance of mine happened to say to me with a smile, 'I saw you shopping in Ramsdens last Saturday.'

'Oh dear, did you?' I replied.

Mary Jean Sinclair

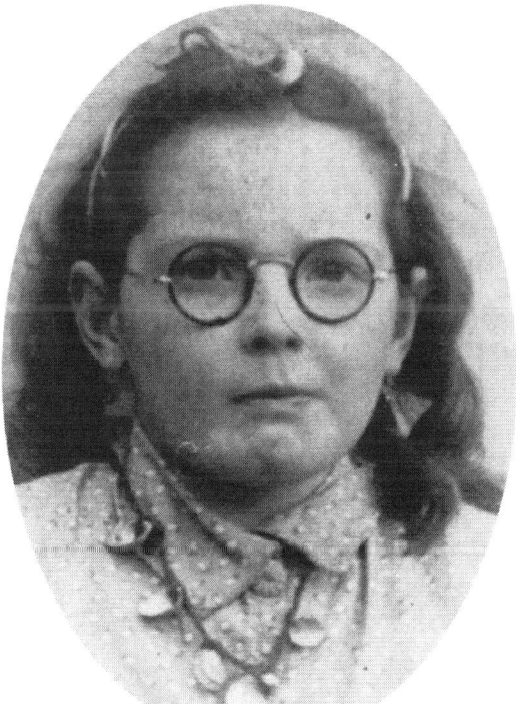

Mary Jean Sinclair   I am

I am the progeny of my parents' love.
A union blessed in Heaven above.
Nurtured at my mother's breast,
A childhood of the very best.

I am the result of both my schools.
Taught to live by all the rules.
Enjoyed the value of words and books,
And not to worry about my looks.

I am the bones of my nursing career.
A job I've always held most dear.
Nursing taught me how to care,
To give and find love everywhere.

I am from the covenant, my husband's wife.
A position I thought was mine for life.
But the oath that long ago we swore
Was broken; I am single once more.

I am the vision of the morning sun;
A whisper of the day just begun;
An ephemeral flutter in a starlit sky,
A tenuous thought to wonder why

I am what I am.

Beginnings

At 2.15 on Tuesday the 25th October, 1938, my brother Robert Anderson Sinclair welcomed his baby sister, Mary Jean. He really wanted a football. By being unable to pronounce 'Mary' he condemned me to a lifetime of having to explain why I was known as 'Jean'. He was the best brother I could wish for, so I forgave him. Granddad was living with us in a small two-bedroomed house, so when I was fourteen months old we moved to a big three-bedroomed house in Park Street, Cleethorpes. The house was long and thin and the backyard had a long path down to the gate which opened onto the alleyway which went from Clerke Street to Johnson Street. I remember sitting in the sun putting bandages on Granddad. I always wanted to be a nurse. Granddad died the next year.

By the time I was eighteen months old I knew all the nursery rhymes. Mam always said I learned how to speak early but I didn't learn how to shut up. On Good Friday I went walkabout. A lady found me wandering down Carr Lane. Apparently, I told her I wouldn't tell her my name and address until she gave me some milk and a biscuit! She then returned me to my distraught mother. Every year this story was repeated with Mam saying it was 'Bad Friday'.

When I was about two Mam was in the alley talking to a neighbour who asked me to take a milk bottle to our front door. I fell over, breaking the bottle and cutting my chin very badly. Nobody nearby had a car, so Mam had to take me on her bike, me clutching a big white towel, to the doctor's house a few streets away. The doctor had been drinking. He sewed my chin up very badly and left me with a scar which was noticeable all my life. Only in old age has it blended in.

In 1941 I was told that if I saved up all the silver paper I could find, I would be able to swap it for a real live baby. Both my parents smoked and inside every packet the cigarettes were enclosed in silver paper. I remember sitting on the stairs clutching my big silver ball waiting for the nurse who was in the front room with my mother. It seemed to take her so long to get the baby out of her bag. Mam kept crying so I guessed she was getting fed up waiting too. I wasn't too sure I wanted to lose my beautiful silver ball but eventually Bob and I were called in to meet baby John David.

During this time of course we were in the middle of the war. Daddy was unable to go in the Navy because he had damaged one eye when he was involved in trying to raise the ships in Scapa Flow. He joined the Home Guard and spent the night out patrolling, putting out fires and rescuing people. He never told us the atrocities he saw. We went into the Morrison shelter each night. This was a large metal crate with mattresses inside. Only once did we have bomb damage when the front door and windows were blown in. My mother was very nervous and as the war was escalating Daddy decided it was too dangerous living so near the docks, so we packed up our things and caught the train to Kirton near Boston to stay with mam's stepsister, Auntie Annie, and family.

Uncle Arthur ran a bakery shop. It was great fun watching the bread being removed from the huge ovens and being in the shop with Auntie Annie selling the bread and cakes. Plus, we always had cakes to eat. Cousin Tess drove a delivery van and often took Bob with her. She didn't like girls. There was a vast cellar under the bakery where the flour et cetera was stored and it was great fun playing under the ground, especially when it was raining, as there were lots of places to hide.

Mammy used to knit all our clothes. I was desperate to learn, and she enjoyed teaching me. We started making a skirt for my dolly, who I had called, very originally, Mary Jean. Being eager when Mam was busy, I decided to show her I could knit on my own. I did a row of knitting very well but it should have been a purl row. I was heartbroken because I thought I had done it wrong, but it became part of the pattern.

My first Christmas there I got a 'nurse' doll. She had a rag body, a pot head and paper eyes with a blue dot in the middle. She had a nurse's apron and hat, and I took her everywhere. John pulled the paper out, so Daddy put a blob of blue paint instead. Daddy also made me a wooden wash tub and clothes wringer. My doll now lives in a shoe box in my cabinet ... a poor bedraggled creature.

Auntie Annie was a very difficult woman to live with. She fell out with my mother and stopped speaking to her. My mother was a lovely lady. She was always kind and polite but very nervous and worried about upsetting people. She was so unhappy that Daddy arranged for us to return home. We were happy to be together again.

School Days: the Start

I was desperate to go back to school. I knew everything my brother knew, and more. The previous year we had been evacuated to Kirton, near Boston and, as it was a small village school, I had been allowed to start with Bob, even though I was too young.

Now we were back in Cleethorpes and my thirst for knowledge was unquenchable. When Bob was five, Mam took us all to Barcroft Street School to enrol him. I told the head that I was coming to school too but was told I would have to wait until I was five. I retorted that if I couldn't start with Bob, I would not be coming at all! But I had to wait.

The day eventually arrived, and I went along to be greeted by forty children of various shapes and sizes, pushing, shoving shouting and boisterous. Worst of all I was the only girl wearing glasses, horrible National Health glasses. I felt small and shy and very scared. It was not a confidence booster to have 'Hey, four-eyes' yelled at you by horrible boys. This was not a very auspicious start to my education. However, the teacher was lovely, and I soon made some friends. The desks were double and I was sat next to a bubbly blonde girl with two pigtails like myself. Olga and I are still the best of friends.

Mammy had taken me on my first day and Bob was supposed to take me after that. He had other ideas and so I took myself and often met up with Jenny from the next street. Jenny and I used to compare our knitting projects and swap patterns. If I was by myself, I would walk along reading as I went. I don't remember learning to read. I don't remember not being able to read.

Lessons were very different from schools today. There was no playing during lessons. We had to learn our times tables by rote and recite them every day and answer random questions. We learnt to read from the 'Janet and John' books and had to take it in turns to read aloud to the class. We would have a story read to us before going home. The playtimes and lunch hour we played in the playground, whatever the weather. At morning break, we each had to drink a third of a pint bottle of milk, given by the government to help disadvantaged children. Most of us hated it. We took it in turns to be milk monitor and make sure all drank it.

Mrs Wordsworth in Year 2 was very strict. Nobody liked her. We all had to be quiet whilst she wrote on the blackboard. One day someone spoke. She turned round and called me out and I was given the cane. I was mortified and furious because it was not me. I was always very quiet and well behaved. You certainly didn't argue with her, but I never forgave her. My right eye had developed a squint about this time and I had to wear a black patch over it. Fortunately, I was confident and it didn't bother me too much when I was now called 'Boss-eyes'. Children really can be so cruel.

My father was a fisherman and was often away at sea for three weeks and only home for a couple of days. He used to sing 'I dream of Jeannie with the light brown hair' to me and I thought he had made it up just for me. The Statutes Fair used to come for a week each year from Nottingham and, one year, Daddy took us all. He gave us each half a crown (30p). The boys took off, but I stayed holding hands with my lovely daddy. He kept asking me if I wanted to go on various rides and I would look at my money and dither and he would say he would pay for me. I got to go on whatever I wanted and went home and put the money in my money box. I loved saving money.

When the weather was nice Mam used to pack up a picnic and meet us from school and we would go over Fuller Street Bridge and play on the beach. We would swim in the sea when the tide was up. We ate sandwiches and drank lukewarm tea. I always thought sandwiches were witches eaten on the sands. We also used to go to Sidney Park where we met our friends and played on the swings and roundabouts. We played hide-and-seek in the bushes and sailed our boats on the pond.

My friend Eleanor used to go to ballet lessons and I was allowed to go, although we didn't have much money. I was in a couple of shows at the Palace and the Theatre Royal. I loved the ballet but didn't really like having to dance on stage. I stopped going when my mother got pregnant as she wasn't very well and I was needed to help at home. I liked doing housework so was more than happy to help with the baking and ironing.

The last year we had to sit the scholarship. Mr Saddington was like a kindly grandfather, tubby but with twinkling blue eyes. He inspired us to do greater things. He once said he would give me sixpence to learn a poem and recite it to the class. *Godfrey Gordon Gustavus Gore* has remained in my memory ever since. He also gave me sixpence because I took *The Life of Florence Nightingale* home and read all 600 pages in the one night. I always had my head in a book. At the end of the year, we all took the eleven-plus exam and it never occurred to me that I wouldn't pass. Most of my friends passed too.

Mam and I had to go to Cleethorpes Girls' Grammar School for an interview with Miss Vallins. I had to find her name and address in the telephone directory, which I had never seen before. She told Mam to make sure I knew the Facts of Life before I started in September. I learned about the birds and the bees walking home down Brereton Avenue.

School Days: Secondary School

Cleethorpes Girls' Grammar School beckoned. With great trepidation I entered those portals of further education, wearing my uniform. Though we were poor, Daddy had given me two big white five-pound notes and Mam and I had visited the upmarket shop to purchase the navy gymslip, blazer, gaberdine mac, beret and navy-and-gold tie. I was so lucky there was enough to buy a brown leather satchel which was de rigeur. Plastic ones screamed 'poverty and exclusion'. I was mixing now with skippers' daughters and other rich people.

The first day we were divided alphabetically into two classes and spent the day collecting books and checking all our uniform had name tapes in. The school was built like a large 'E'. The classrooms were the outer part and all looked out of floor-to-ceiling windows, onto a walkway surrounding grass quadrangles. The middle contained the hall, gym and administrative offices including the head's office. We all had a desk – and the various teachers came to us for lessons. We had science labs, an art room and domestic science rooms.

We worked hard and had homework every night. I loved the academic work but hated sports. Prefects strutted around checking we were behaving. No walking on the grass and, if you were caught out without your beret on, that warranted a dreaded visit to Miss Vallins. She was a slim, elegant virago who put the fear of God in us if we were in trouble, but actually was a very nice teacher. She had trained at the ladies' college in Bedford and impressed upon us that we were all to behave like ladies and that 'ladies perspire, horses sweat'.

Having settled into my school regime, my mother informed me she was pregnant. She had been to the doctor's because she was not feeling well and kept fainting. His advice was for her to get pregnant to 'sort out her hormones'. I was ecstatic. Unfortunately, Mam was not at all well whilst she was pregnant, so my brother and I had to take over looking after the family. Bob did the shopping and fires and I did the cooking and cleaning. I loved being a little housewife.

Mam had the double bed brought down into the front room and she wanted a new pink candlewick bedspread. I was duly despatched to Petchells and successfully purchased it. Standing behind me was a lady who also wanted a pink one and I had bought the last one. 'Wait a minute, madam,' he said and proceeded to persuade me my mother would be just as happy with a gold one. I was furious. I may have been only eleven, but I took my parcel and left. A Sinclair stare can kill at three feet!

My beautiful baby sister was born on Saturday February 18th, 1950. I really knew nothing about how a baby was born. It had been a difficult birth. Mam developed phlebitis of both legs and the treatment in those days was bed rest. This lasted for three months and the lady who was booked to look after us had to go because we couldn't afford to pay her. My mother really had no friends, so we all learned to look after everything as well as going to school. We coped amazingly well.

After Mam was on her feet again it was obvious that Margaret was not a thriving child. She struggled to feed and kept throwing a temperature every couple of weeks for no known reason. Mam spent a lot of nights walking the floor with her. After Margaret had her own child at twenty-one, it was discovered she had a heart problem which had gone undiagnosed.

When Margaret was eighteen months old and being healthier, Mam told me she was pregnant again. I was furious. I didn't want Mam to go through such an awful time again. Once more we were plunged into looking after everything as well as Margaret, who slept with me to give Mam a rest. It was another long difficult pregnancy, but we survived.

Two years and ten days after Margaret was born, we had another sister. The delivery was even worse, and Mam was so ill they had to send for the flying squad who put up a drip. She refused to go into hospital. My dad had been able to stay at home with us for a week or so but if he didn't go to sea, we didn't have any money. On the day that he was going off to sea he sat crying with me asking me to look after Mam. He did not want to go but had to. I only found out after he died that my mother was his second wife and that his first wife had died in childbirth and the little boy died at nine months. No wonder he was crying. They were devoted to each other, and he was a brilliant dad. Mam slowly recovered.

We got there in the end, but I resented Christine for a long time and although I loved her, I had such a strong bond with Margaret. We used to dress them both the same and they were such pretty little babies.

I was doing all right at school. Looking back, I could have been brilliant if I had put in more effort, but I got by very well and was so involved with my sisters and even made their clothes and knitted for them. I think the highlight of my school career was when we went to London to see *Macbeth* at The Old Vic which we were studying for our GCEs. We were taken on a guided tour round London and then round the Houses of Parliament. Our annual holidays consisted of a day trip to Skegness with the 'Lumpers Club' which was run for dockers, and which Dad saved up for all year.

It was a great adventure before the hard work of our exams, which I passed.

All Aboard the *Flying Scotsman*

No one slept that night. We were all too excited. First thing in the morning we were catching the *Flying Scotsman* at Grimsby Station to travel to Edinburgh. I had never been to a big city and as we spent the afternoon walking down Princes' Street the big shops were amazing. We saw the pretty gardens including the Floral Clock which was very famous.

We boarded the *St Magnus* to take us on the next leg of our journey to Aberdeen. We sailed overnight and arrived there in the early morning. During the day we explored the town and saw all the big buildings made from granite which twinkled in the sunshine. The final journey was overnight again, and we arrived in Kirkwall.

My father had left Orkney in 1928 and this trip, nearly twenty years later, was his first time back. It was so expensive to travel and he had been saving up for a long time. We were met by Uncle Billy, who was the youngest and lived at home with his mother. He was a thin, stooped little man and always had a pipe in his mouth. He had a bad chest so couldn't do hard work. He wore baggy brown trousers with a white shirt and tie under a brown waistcoat. He had a car and was the taxi driver for the island. There weren't many cars on the islands.

It seemed a long way to St Margaret's Hope in South Ronaldsay. Before the First World War all the islands were separate but during the war the Italian prisoners of war were made to construct a barrier linking the mainland to Burray and to South Ronaldsay and we travelled over these. It was quite scary because the water lapped up on either side and at high tides came over the road.

We were to stay with Auntie Maggie and cousin Chrissie in 'Roselea'. Auntie Maggie was a little round lady with twinkling brown eyes. She always seemed to be smiling. She and Chrissie both liked baking and we always had lovely cakes after meals. All the fresh air gave us children an appetite.

Granny lived across the road in a little house. She slept downstairs. She was a tiny bird-like lady. Her hair was pulled tightly to the back, secured in a bun with a middle parting. She wore a long black dress under a big white pinny. Her face was a petite heart-shape and she looked very severe. We all had difficulty understanding what she said because she spoke with a broad Orcadian dialect.

Everywhere we went my parents towered over everyone. My dad was a tall, blond, blue-eyed Adonis. He looked like the Duke of Edinburgh. My mother was tall, slim and very elegant. She was a very calming, loving presence. We were greeted always as 'wee Jimmock frae the mill hoose and his English lady'. Whisky flowed freely and tea and cakes for the ladies and us. The harbour master at the Hope pier was a half-brother of Dad.

Uncle Harry, Chrissie's husband, was in charge of Kirkwall Airport so we went there to see a couple of little planes fly off. He was tall and had a very red face. I found out later that he was an alcoholic, had been a soldier stationed in Orkney and married Chrissie and never went back to Wales. They had a gorgeous little girl, Wilma, and I loved playing with her. Marjory was Auntie Maggie's niece and was fourteen. She thought she knew it all and tried to boss us about … the only bad thing about Orkney!

We were taken to the east side of South Ronaldsay to the little ruin where Dad had been born. Mary Ann lived in this tiny mill house with four of her six children. Her eldest, Robert Anderson, emigrated to New Zealand and Mary Jane trained as a nurse, married and went to Australia. Auntie Maggie married Will. Uncle Peter lived in Cleethorpes. John was drowned when he was twenty-one at sea. After Grandad died in 1921, she moved into Roselea. There was one room downstairs and to go upstairs you had to go out the front door and round the side to climb up the stone steps to the bedroom. The house was on the seashore and at high tide the water came up to the front door. I cannot imagine what it was like in the long bleak winters.

Dad's family had lived in this area since at least 1621. The church was just above The Mill House and all his relatives were buried in the graveyard there. We managed to find a stone for Granddad and his parents, who had a big cross with their names on it. Grandad was one of ten children, eight of whom survived. No wonder so many people knew Dad. If only I had asked more questions, my later genealogical journey would have been much easier.

It was strange having Dad with us all the time and we really enjoyed being a complete family. We even got Dad to go in the sea with us which he would never do at home. He could swim very well. He was quite shy but could be funny. His favourite saying was that when Mam was forty he could swap her for two twenty-year-olds. Mam would just laugh and say, 'Jim.' Mam was always busy at home, so it was lovely for her to have a rest.

The water was so clear you could see your feet on the sands below and the sands were golden. The sky seemed to go on forever and we had glorious sunshine the whole month we were there. We went to lots of beaches, and they were all quiet and we had them to ourselves.

All too soon it was time to return home. Uncle Billy took us to the *St Rognvald* to sail to Aberdeen. As Mam really hated being at sea, we left the boat at Aberdeen and came home by train.

Three weeks later Granny died.

Pam Smith

Pam Smith **Where I'm From**

I am from the ancient Celts who settled long ago in Wales,
A land of barren mountains and green and verdant vales.
I am from a mining village where coal was once the master.
The mine now closed, forgotten, buried under bricks and plaster.

Then blackened men deep underground hacked coal and risked their lives
Encased in dust, in hobnailed boots trudged homewards to their wives.
Their terraced homes were poor enough, but that's not where wealth lies,
Contentment and community gives joy that sparkles eyes.

Saturdays the rugby team would take on a neighbouring side
They finished filthy, torn and tattered, but winning gave such pride.
Sundays, after chapel, they practised for the concert of the year,
And the music that they made was like velvet on the ear.

The womenfolk were homemakers, trips to Cardiff such a treat.
Their pride a well-scrubbed step, and to hang out the whitest sheet.
No gadgets, just hard graft, a scrubbing board, fingers cracked and sore,
Wet Mondays meant washing hung in the kitchen, dripping on the floor.

Such a close-knit band who lived, laughed, and sometimes died together,
Holidays were carnivals, street teas, often in wet Welsh weather.
But no one travelled abroad those days to try to find the sun
For who would want to go away when the village had such fun.

With war came the life and death struggle to keep our homeland free,
Our doors were opened wide to welcome each tearful evacuee.
When I left my village that like a womb had cushioned me
I realised my birthplace had forged my identity.

Beginnings

From the age of four, in the charge of my older sister, I walked a mile and back to school through Llanharan, my small Welsh village. As there were no school dinners, I did this twice a day. The main road passed through the village square, over the railway bridge, winding its way past my house and up a hill which was lined with terraced houses and where eyes behind lace curtains monitored the comings and goings. Mrs Marlin lived there and she was a nosy-parker but her rendering of 'The Old Rugged Cross' left everyone moist-eyed. My best friend, Millie, lived next door to Mrs Marlin but Millie who was eight, like me, and her three sisters, attended the Roman Catholic School in the next village and I was so envious of them as they went to their school on a bus.

Once over the hill the road levelled out with yet more terraced houses and small shops but the shop that drew us like a magnet was Mrs Sheen's toy shop where we dallied, with noses pressed against the window, gazing at the amazing assortment of toys, dolls, popguns and kites; Mrs Sheen would have won no prizes for window dressing.

We would hurry on past the allotments and pigeon lofts where clouds of feathered beauties swooped over our heads and we whispered as we walked by the intimidating grey walls, crowned with barbed wire, that hid the coal mine. Soon the pavement led us along a hedge where red campions, primroses and tiny violets peeped through the grassy bank and we could see the school. School was a squat, red-brick building behind black railings and I always shuddered when it came into view as it was not a happy place. In the reception class I was put in charge of the classroom door, a clever move as I was probably the only child likely to escape through it.

Was there anything remarkable about my village? It began as a small settlement nestling where the Vale of Glamorgan gave way to the rugged Brecon Beacons. There was an old stone church, a village square, a smithy and a squire who lived in an imposing manor called Ty Mawr (big house) which had been built on the proceeds of slavery. On a clear day if you climbed the mountain behind the church you could see the Bristol Channel some five miles away as the crow flies. A small brook tumbled through the ferns and bracken where sure-footed sheep made well-trodden tracks and the silence was broken by the tinkling of skylarks.

With the coming of the railways towards the end of the eighteenth century the village was on the map as trains steamed through en route between London and Pembroke and, early in the nineteenth century, a rich seam of anthracite coal was discovered and hence the coal mine and black pyramids arrived with housing for the incoming miners.

When mothers said, 'I'm busy, you go out to play,' as mothers did then, I would cross the road, go over the small bridge and perch on the bank of the prettiest little brook that snaked, gurgling, through the village, it was the Ewenny Fach, clear sparkling water, quite shallow but fast flowing as it sped under the small bridge. Where it had been ducted under the railway it had become a small pond where brown trout lazed, safe behind the railings from fishermen or marauding small boys learning the art of trout tickling (this art involved sliding a hand under the bank where a trout might be hiding and the tickling action seemed to mesmerise the trout, which could then be hauled out for someone's supper). Along the bank I knew where there were pools of still water, home to small brown minnows, transparent and almost invisible against the sandy riverbed. I would watch and swoop, scooping sand, minnow and water into a jar to see how many I could catch before putting them all back. It was all very friendly.

Such was the brook on balmy summer days, but winter brought a different scenario; trickling through snow-covered banks it made a Christmas scene, serene and beautiful, but Wales knows heavy rainfall. Clouds grey with moisture sweep across the Atlantic and before rising over the Brecon Beacons, they deposit their contents as torrential rain. I well remember a very wet October which began with heavy rain which went on for days. When would it stop? The brook roared along like an enraged dragon gushing, brown and angry, through the village.

Everywhere was wet. Pavements disappeared. Drains gave up the unequal struggle of coping with the inexhaustible deluge. And still it rained. Floodwater, brown and muddy, covered the roads and crept into the little terraced houses. Wellingtons were the only footwear and children splashed happily in the recreation ground where rugby posts stood sentinel over the sodden pitch.

As I left school on a grey afternoon when it wasn't exactly raining, just a heavy drizzle in the air – a very Welsh phenomenon – a small boy with his mother was kicking and splashing where the pavement should have been. He was full of energy and ran ahead of his mother far too near the fast-flowing water. His mother called out to him but as he turned with a cheeky grin, he lost his footing and fell headlong where the water was swirling in furious circles as it tried to flow under the bridge. The current had claimed the child before he had a chance to call out. He had just disappeared. I stared disbelievingly and the mother howled in anguish, calling the little boy's name.

'Wynne! Wynne!' she screamed. 'Mummy's here, I'm coming to get you,' and she paddled in a short distance but there was only swirling water.

People came running and stared helplessly. Two village men tried valiantly to wade in holding onto a thick rope, but the current swept them off their feet. The Fire Brigade formed a chain across the water but could not locate the child and with bowed heads said they would try when the water had receded.

The crowd, shocked and silent, many openly crying, dispersed and I watched with my mother from the front window of our house. The village policeman put his arm around the sobbing mother and escorted her away.

The water slowly receded and the child's body, which had been trapped under the bridge, was recovered and, in such a close-knit community where triumphs and traumas are shared, the village grieved with the family and the child's dreadful death will not be forgotten. Somehow, I no longer felt at ease with the Ewenny Fach. That October afternoon haunted me, and I spent more time with my friend Millie, or perhaps I was just growing up.

School Days

'Now who will I choose to look after the door today?'

I sat, a tear-stained four-year-old in the reception class, desperately wanting my mum and eyeing the door with a view to escaping through it.

'Pamela, you can be door monitor,' and with that Miss Griffiths, lame and with tightly curled grey hair, put a red sash over my head which probably said 'Door Monitor' except that I couldn't read.

Sitting next to me in the classroom was Hazel Coleman whose father delivered our milk. Hazel had red hair, lots of freckles, a constantly runny nose and a continual sniff which I found very distasteful. In the afternoon we were given tubs of beads and pieces of string, rather like shoelaces, and the activity of threading the beads was to improve our coordination but I would not share with Hazel. There were big glassy beads like marbles and small sparkly beads which were quite difficult to pick up. I sat and watched and Miss Griffiths asked, 'Pamela, why aren't you threading beads like the other children?'

I dissolved into tears as I couldn't tell her that Hazel's runny nose had made the beads sticky. Miss Griffiths called me a 'cry baby' and I howled even louder.

On returning to school after Christmas, 1940 had arrived and I had learned how to write my name, although I often unwittingly wrote it as Map. With the New Year came an influx of evacuees.

A school from London was evacuated to our Welsh village and the war had changed our lives forever. The classroom windows were criss-crossed with sticky brown tape: it was wintertime and there were no streetlights and all windows had to be fitted with blackout curtains or shutters, as not a sliver of light must show or German bombers would know where we were. I hid my head under the pillow at night in fear. It was a dark world. The docks at Cardiff were constantly being targeted in German raids and words like 'Nazi' became synonymous with 'nasty' and I really believed that German measles was an affliction from the dreaded Germans.

During playtime at school the girls played on a small, grassed area, the boys in the yard and the evacuees in the big, football field. Some of the girls had older sisters who probably taught them the popular songs of the day and I desperately tried to sing along to 'You Are My Sunshine' and 'Red Sails in the Sunset' but I was probably a few words behind. Brenda Thomas knew all the words. How I envied her. During the school day there were air raid warnings when the siren at the local coal mine would wail and we took shelter in private houses until the blasts of the all-clear meant that we could return to school.

My grandfather, Geca, was too old for active service and was an air raid warden. One dark night a bomb meant for Cardiff was dropped on a small bungalow, luckily unoccupied, and a huge crater appeared in the road. Geca cordoned it off and stood guard to redirect any traffic and it was not until dawn that a cat ran across the crater and he realised that he had been guarding a mound of soot from the stricken bungalow. How we teased him.

When I was eleven I took the Scholarship Examination and continued my education at Bridgend Girls' Grammar School eight miles away. It meant travelling by train. The prospect of travelling by train out of my comfort zone worried me and my pride was hurt when my mother asked Brian, who was two years my senior and lived along my road, to look after me. I was both grateful and mortified.

My heart sank when I had the first glimpse of Bridgend Girls' Grammar School through an avenue of trees: a forbidding, grey-stone building and the word prison came into my mind. My classroom windows were too high to see through and the headmistress's office was just next to my classroom. I had a sense of gloom and, coming from a village school where I knew most people, I found myself with thirty complete strangers. Miss Williams, my class teacher, was a pleasant middle-aged lady but all too often we heard the harsh voice of Miss Evans, the headmistress, and my heart would race. Miss Evans's hair was scraped back into a severe bun and she had piercing eyes that were magnified behind horn-rimmed spectacles; with a hairy tweed suit and brogue shoes she reigned supreme and terrified me.

Morning breaks and lunchtimes were the highlights of the day when I joined a group playing football on the hockey field. I excelled at football and glorified at being chosen first for teams and scoring goals, but it was to be short lived. The games teacher complained that the hockey field was becoming a mud bath and football was banned. Those of us who were still missing the exercise took the wooden benches from around the field and built high jumps, balancing beams, even a long jump, and it was great fun until Miss Evans got wind of it. We had organised a high-jump competition and were completely absorbed with it and even our audience had not noticed Miss Evans's arrival. Everything stopped. There was total uncomfortable silence. I quickly pulled down my gymslip which I had tucked into my knicker legs to facilitate high jumping. Miss Evans rounded on me. I was quivering and biting my bottom lip in fear, but she assumed I was smiling. She seemed to grow in stature as she spat out her words.

'What do you think you are doing? Take that smirk off your face. You wouldn't be smirking if you had fallen and broken your leg! Put all these benches back and wait for me outside my office.'

I shrank under the onslaught but with that she flounced off.

Feeling sick, I stood outside the office, my mouth dry, my legs wobbly. The bell for afternoon lessons clanged and the corridor filled with girls who threw me pitying glances. The corridor emptied and in the silence I heard the heavy tread of brogue shoes but kept my head low.

'Why aren't you at your lessons?'

'You t-t-told me to wait outside your office, Miss Evans,' I stuttered.

The telephone began to ring in the office and Miss Evans felt in her pocket for the key to her room. I was rooted to the spot and trying not to cry. 'Well, hurry along then, what did you say your name was?'

'Pamela David,' I whispered but with that Miss Evans shot into her office to answer the telephone and, feeling a great weight lifted off my shoulders, I crept back into my classroom, where I was the focus of thirty curious glances. Phew! Saved by the bell.

A Special Person

Perhaps all Welshmen are meant to be short, dark haired and of stocky build, for my father fitted that description and his six younger brothers were cast in the same mould; typical Celts, although Dad's hair was prematurely white and usually hidden under his trilby hat which seemed a permanent fixture on his head. Dad had piercing grey eyes and a quiet demeanour but a presence suggesting that he would 'take no nonsense', probably because he had always disciplined his brothers as my grandfather had little authority over his sons and spent much of his time at the Welsh Baptist Chapel. With any physical activity that required concentrated energy Dad would screw his face into a grimace that looked as if he had bitten into a particularly sour lemon.

Dad was born Joseph Aaran David in 1908 in the small mining village of Brynna that nestled in the hillside on the edge of the Vale of Glamorgan before the hillside rose rapidly to become the Brecon Beacons. The David family had lived in the area for generations, as Dad jokingly said, 'Since they crawled out of the sea.'

He was the first child of a family of shopkeepers, with a grocery shop, a barber's shop, a chip shop and a billiard hall – billiards then was a very popular pastime – this was a time before radios or even electricity had entered most homes. My paternal grandmother had three children in a very short space of time and, as my father was prone to putting clothes pegs on the babies' noses, he was sent to live with his paternal grandparents. Welsh was the spoken language, but children were not allowed to speak Welsh in school and that sounded the death knell of the Welsh language, something that my father deeply regretted. Dad was a bright child and passed his Scholarship Examination to attend a grammar school but chose not to go and left school at fourteen to work in the family business. This was the time of the Great Depression and there was real hardship in South Wales that Dad never forgot.

From an early age Dad's imagination had been fired by the motor car and somehow, despite the Depression, his grandparents bought him a car. In the 1930s he realised his dream and opened a garage, even though there were very few cars on the road. In the early days it was a struggle as money was short and he was married with a wife and two small children, but he and my mother battled on. He liked nothing better than delving into a car engine so that his hands always bore evidence of engine grease, and when he picked me up his clothes smelt of garage and petrol. The local mine was struggling to stay solvent, and Dad became a coal merchant with lorries selling coal from the local mine in nearby Cardiff and Barry, selling it a little cheaper to help keep the local mine working.

With the coming of the war in 1939 Dad was busier than ever. Parts for vehicles were impossible to get and he worked late into the night to keep essential vehicles on the road. Men were called for the three armed services so there were fewer drivers for the coal lorries, but coal was the only means of heating homes and the lorries were often working well into the evening and driving in the darkness with two layers of newspaper over the headlights to comply with war-time regulations. One of Dad's war-time jobs, which caused great amusement, was to transport the midwife. Most babies seemed to arrive in the night but Dad never complained. He was also an air raid warden for which he was provided with a uniform and a hard metal hat. I'm not sure if it ever replaced the trilby but my sister and I enjoyed marching up and down wearing it.

My dad was very committed to his village and the people who lived there and when the war ended in 1945 he was persuaded to stand for election for District Councillor. South Wales was traditionally a Labour stronghold and my father was staunchly independent and would vote according to his principles rather than be told how to vote, however he was elected and had really found his niche and loved the many commitments, meetings, magistrate sessions, conferences. We rarely saw him. My mother wanted to send my sister and me to a private school in Cardiff, but Dad was horrified and said that he had gone to the local school with the local people and his children would go to school with their children. When we heard that the Coronation would be televised my sister and I hassled Dad to buy a television. They were very expensive and very few people that we knew had bought one. Dad relented and bought two, putting one in the village hall so that everyone could watch the Coronation.

Dad didn't go to church or chapel but he had real empathy with people, he had little respect for money and less for people with 'airs and graces'. I often told him that he was an 'inverted snob'; he was his own man and nothing would change him and he earned respect because of it.

When I left home to go to university my father was standing for County Councillor for the Vale of Glamorgan but this was a much bigger area and whether he would win was debatable. Mobile phones were still a figment of the imagination in the 1950s and I received a telegram which said, 'Dad topped the pole!' How we laughed! It meant further commitments for both him and my mother. He became Chairman of the Education Committee and was instrumental in bringing Welsh schools back into the area.

On the occasion of his opening the new Welsh comprehensive school my mother happened to be opening a bazaar and arrived at the ceremony as Dad was delivering his speech on stage. As ever, she had dutifully put out all his clothes and cleaned his shoes but had left before he had dressed. Quite how she could possibly have known was something we all puzzled over as she announced, 'I could see that he hadn't changed his vest.' How could she have known?

Dad had one great fault. Most of us have an inbuilt clock, but not Dad. He had to be chivvied to get to meetings on time and his lateness often drove my mother to distraction. The house clocks were always ten or more minutes fast but if he was running too late to change for County Hall meetings he would put on a white muffler, an overcoat and the inevitable trilby, grab his briefcase and set off. Dad was president of the rugby club for thirty years and when opening the new rugby club in the village he presented them with a clock which caused great amusement. Dad's response was, 'Better Joe David late, than the late Joe David.'

On his death hundreds of people attended his funeral and the rugby club choir sang his favourite hymn, 'Calon Lan', which means, 'A Happy Heart', but they sang it in Welsh, of course.

A Producer's Perils

How can an examining board, sitting in the front row of a theatre, disappear in a white cloud? Well, we did it. 'We' being the Spalding Gang Show, and it happened on the evening when we were being assessed by the Big Wigs, the examining team from London and we were desperate that they would consider our show had reached the required standard to be awarded the coveted red Gang Show scarf. The gang, scouts, guides, brownies, cubs and leaders had been rehearsing for months, our costumes all sewn, lines all perfect, and more money than we could really afford invested in lighting and props.

I arrived at the theatre far too early, butterflies in my stomach and checking everything I had already checked. The hall was eerily quiet until the gang began to filter in and then there was no time for jangling nerves. Cubs were first with the make-up team as they had to be in the first half of the show because of age restrictions and they were dressed in pink polka-dot dresses and curly wigs for a Shirley Temple number, rather incongruous with their football boots. Yet as each was given rosy cheeks, freckles and cupid-bow lips the screams of laughter set my teeth on edge. I felt sick.

The team from London arrived and were escorted to the front row. The curtains opened to a rousing favourite, 'We're riding along on the crest of a wave', with actions that had been practised to perfection. The Londoners looked suitably impressed.

The next item on the programme was a dance number which required some mist to give a mystic effect. A fog machine was beyond our resources and a scout squatted behind the curtains with a bucket of dry ice and a jug of water with instructions to drip a little water onto the ice and waft the mist over the stage. The dancers tripped onto the stage to the jaunty music, but with a sudden sizzling sound the dancers, London team and musical director all disappeared in a cloud of white fog. I felt my way to the place where the scout had been squatting and as the cloud thinned, I could see that he had poured the entire contents of the jug of water onto the ice. There was laughter from the audience and a voice from the front row chirped, 'Well, it's cleaner than our London smog!'

The scout was replaced for further shows by a scouter and the rest of the show continued without a hitch. We were awarded the red scarf with 'Spalding Gang Show' in bold yellow lettering, a scarf that we all wore with great pride.

I had never heard of gang shows until I received a letter asking if my brownie unit would like to be involved in a gang show that the Spalding Scout Movement were planning. The Guide Commissioner said caustically that left to the scouts it would never happen but, of course, all the brownies jumped up and down at the prospect of being on stage and I found myself taking them to a rehearsal at a local school. I sat in the foyer waiting for them and keeping a low profile when the scout leader who was in charge of the rehearsal dashed out, red faced, thrust a wad of printed sheets in my hand and gasped, 'I've a really important phone call to make so please could you hear them through their lines?' With that he disappeared. The title on the printed sheets said, *Fairy Tales and Nursery Rhymes* and, dutifully, I heard them through their lines.

The following week it was assumed that I would continue and, bit by bit, it was, 'Can you check their costumes for the finale?' and, 'Will you sort the scout sketch?' I realised that I had surreptitiously been drawn into the production team and eventually became the Producer.

The first night of our very first show was fast approaching, and the dress rehearsal was in the new Spalding Hall of the Civic Centre; it held an audience of 500 with a stage far larger than any of the school stages that the cast had used and there were elegant, rose-pink velvet curtains. But what a disaster! Both brownies and cubs froze with stage fright, they became tongue-tied and shuffled backwards away from the lights, the Musical Director strummed on the piano in frustration, the stage crew were late with scene changes, even the most reliable senior members muffed their lines.

Somewhat subdued, the last of the gang left and the production team stood wondering how it could have been so bad when we suddenly realised that our feet were wet and water was cascading from the stage into the hall. The caretaker had been hovering and waiting to lock up and we soon found him as he came rushing in, cursing, 'Those little hooligans have been messing with them sprinklers ...' Somehow the sprinklers had been activated but the switch was far too high for our 'little hooligans'; the switch was probably caught as the stage crew were moving scenery at the end of the rehearsal.

The very first night arrived, the stage had dried out but there was a tell-tale water mark on the rose-pink velvet curtains. I read through the programme for the fifth time. Parents, scout and guide groups filled the hall and the cast were bubbling with excitement. There were 180 on stage for the opening number, and, as the curtains opened, there was a burst of clapping from the audience as the lights picked out the startlingly white T-shirts with 'Spalding Gang' splashed across the front in red lettering.

The gang sang well, concentration etched on their faces, and I stood in the wings holding a large sign that said 'Smile', but as the show progressed they relaxed into enjoying the clapping and the audience approval and I could put my sign away. To my amazement, the show was running smoothly. The 'piece de resistance' was the finale which did almost 'bring the house down'. As the lights dimmed the gang disappeared behind a screen of white sheets that had been hidden behind their backs and, by means of the projector at the back of the hall, ships of the Royal Navy sailed across the screen as the gang sang, 'Meet the Navy'. The audience roared their approval and Gang Show was well and truly launched in Spalding. 'When can we do the next?' was the cry as the gang, buoyed with their success, bounced off the stage with the new-found confidence that even the most timid shared.

There were many more years of Gang Show and so many talented youngsters, like Adrian, who with bowler hat and walking stick became Charlie Chaplin under the flashing strobe light. In one scout sketch the camp cook had eggs hidden under his hat but in dubbing him 'Sir Cook' the eggs were broken and trickled down his face. Thinking that he had found a solution the 'cook' blew some eggs and filled them with his mother's egg shampoo. The expression on his face as the shampoo ran into his eyes was one of acute agony and with eyes tightly closed, he was led off stage to the cloakroom. That scout is now a successful businessman in the town, but I smile when I remember his undignified exit.

My brownie pack had perfected a musical number where they were dressed as bedraggled fairies living in a very neglected garden. The first bars of the music rang out but no fairies had appeared. 'Play it again,' I hissed from behind the curtains as five of the seventeen arrived. 'It's Rachel,' one whispered, 'she's lying on the stairs crying because she's broken her wings and we can't get past.' One by one they clambered over Rachel and rescued the situation. Children rarely let you down.

I did meet Ralph Reader who staged the first Gang Show, in London. It was his eightieth birthday and Whitley Bay Scout Group had put on an amazing show in his honour. I told him that Spalding Gang Show had given some of the most unlikely and shy children the opportunity to shine. The parents of one little girl with spina bifida tearfully told me what being included in the 'gang' had meant to their daughter; she had not stopped smiling and singing the gang show songs until she died from complications of her condition.

Sadly, and for a variety of reasons, Gang Show could not continue in Spalding and there was a huge gap in our calendars and in our lives. At the last show the finale was a Ralph Reader number, 'We've been making memories for a long, long, long time' and I have so many memories that make me smile and that I share with old Gang Show members when our paths cross. The Civic Centre has been redesigned so that the Spalding Hall no longer exists, and I wonder what became of the beautiful rose-pink curtains with the water mark?

Pat Sieling

Pat Sieling   Where I'm From

I am from the land of the midnight sun,
From the dust of my ancestors,
How I would have loved to sail in a longboat
To travel to far-off lands,
To taste the atmosphere around me
To know their intimate way of life.

I am from across the sea
From far-off shores where elk and deer ran free
Where the North winds blew
In harsh and rugged lands many years ago
I am from warriors, fighters and hunters of the sea.

I am from the bold and courageous
Of bearded men and warrior maidens
From a ruthless cutthroat nation
Trying to break free, to be me.

Beginnings

Cast your mind back to the 1940s, Britain was at war with Germany, food was in short supply and times were hard for everyone.

I was born in 1943 in a small market town called Dunstable in the county of Bedfordshire, in a room above my granddad's cobbler's shop, the only child of Jack and Joan Kirtley. In those days life was very different to life as you know it today. Before the war my family were members of a very tight-knit community.

My father tried six times to get into the RAF but his flat feet let him down every time. The theory behind his rejection was that if he had the misfortune to be shot down behind enemy lines his feet would stop him from running and making a swift escape. Before the war broke out, he worked for Hadley Page in Luton, making parts for small aircraft, so this stood him in good stead for repairing damaged war-time aircraft. He moved temporarily to Swindon and became an engineer doing just that.

Mother was a professional dancer before war broke out but a change in career beckoned to her as well. Manpower was low in many areas one being the local fire service. They were desperate for someone to work on their switchboard and that person was Mum.

This was a relatively rural area. My favourite farmers were George and Kath from Rye Farm in Eaton Bray with their two daughters, Brenda and Jackie. I loved helping them mix pig feed and collect eggs. One day I was given a chick of my own I named Daisy, however after months of tender care she fell into our outside loo and drowned. I was devastated but trying to keep a chicken in a small, shared yard with two outside toilets was really not a good idea.

During the early stages of my life, we lived with my grandparents in West Street in their 400-year-old property with Granddad's cobbler's shop at the front where a living room used to be. We had a coal cellar beneath the quaint building with no garden but the yard with two outside toilets shared with our neighbours who had a sweet shop. The floor in the kitchen, or parlour as we called it, was on a slope. You opened a small wooden door to go up the twisting stairs to two small bedrooms and a landing which was known as my bedroom, so you went through my room to access the other two. One sitting room where we had a piano, radio, an open fireplace and just a couple of comfy chairs with a cupboard that ran the whole length behind the fireplace – very handy for airing clothes. We had no bathroom, so baths were in a tin bath in front of the fire. My playground was Granddad's shop, where I used to pull a box round as a doll's pram and breathe in the wonderful smell of fresh leather from the sheaths hanging from the ceiling. The aroma will stay with me forever.

Granddad Victor Percy was a real character, born in 1888 with polio which caused him to be a disabled person all his life. A jolly chap, he never complained about anything. He had a pipe always in his mouth, and nothing stopped him walking to his local pub the Plume of Feathers every night for his pint of beer, even during an air raid.

Grandma Hepzibah was so different, organised and clever. She ran the local WRVS for the Civil Defence and a penny a week fund for the Red Cross and St John's Ambulance Service, receiving a letter from the Duke of Gloucester thanking her for her war efforts. She was responsible for billeting refugees that came to us from London – of which there were many – often with just the clothes on their backs.

In particular, I remember two refugees, a mother and son from Holland. They managed to escape the Nazis and fled to London, eventually to us in Bedfordshire. I always had my suspicions that the mother had something to do with the Dutch resistance movement and had to flee to avoid capture. They were so grateful that a friendship between the Dutch lady and my mother lasted for decades. It was during this time that the London docks were bombed; I heard that townsfolk could read their newspapers in the centre of town by the light of the fires.

There is another great story about the young German airman based at the Dunstable Glider Club learning to fly prior to war breaking out. Granddad repaired their boots, and these young men were so taken with the way all the local shopkeepers had looked after them they promised that if war ever did break out, they would never bomb the centre of our town, and guess what, they never did. They turned at the local hospital away from us.

Sunday morning was always Sunday school to learn about Jesus and to teach us kids to be good and kind. I have a treasured book called *Sally and the Hare* presented to me for the best attendance. I really don't think that was hard to achieve as the Baptist Church was right next door to our shop.

Sunday afternoons were spent with Granddad driving to the villages to return farmers' boots they had left with us on market day to be repaired. No money was ever exchanged. Payment was always in chickens, rabbits, ducks or eggs. Grandma was never too happy about this. I remember her shouting, 'Victor, how can I pay our bills with these?'

His answer was always, 'Well, woman, we won't go hungry now, will we?' They were both great characters.

Sunday evenings, Granddad moved the furniture and we had a pretend day out, always to Southend-on-Sea in his big armchair. Then the day came I was carried on Granddad's shoulders to our town hall to hear the proclamation that war was finally over.

School Days

Everything was changing for Mum, Dad and me. Moving day arrived and we were on our way to this development on the outskirts of town, almost, you would be forgiven in thinking, to the country. We had fields either side of us and the Chiltern Hills behind with the local steam railway chugging merrily between Luton and Dunstable, moving workers from one place to another. Our new house was part built pre-war, but then after the war a licence had to be obtained from the local council for a builder to purchase materials to finish it. We moved in with two deck chairs, a table, beds and a new kitten called Timmy.

1948 heralded a new start for all of us; new jobs for Mum and Dad, a new house and I was about to start primary school. I could finally pack away my Mickey Mouse gas mask that frightened our former neighbour's cat. We had moved away from post war Dunstable with the hustle and bustle of the cattle market in the market square on Wednesdays where local famers bought and sold their cattle, exchanging tales of the olden days. The street market had also reopened twice a week selling everything from furniture to buttons and bows. This is where our dressmaker Mrs Bird bought all her materials. She was a wonderful, talented lady but my mother always insisted that I had coats, hats, dresses and knickers with a pocket in for my handkerchief, all to match. I hated it!

The day came; I walked across the fields with Mum and stepped into my first school wearing my smart red-and-grey uniform. Feeling a little nervous, but excited at the same time, I remember thinking how big everything was – the buildings, the teachers and, oh, the endless corridors and classrooms went on and on; a place where you could easily get lost and yes, you guessed it, I often did. We all said goodbye to our parents and were ushered inside and shown where to hang our coat and PE bag with our new black plimsolls which were the forerunner of trainers.

Our form Teacher was Miss Pepperill, or as we very disrespectfully called her, old Pepperpot, but only when we thought she couldn't hear us. She told us to all go to the toilet and rejoin our class. Well, this was my first big mistake. You see, I got locked in the loo and no amount of yelling and banging on the door could alert my fellow classmates or my teacher. Left sobbing and feeling so alone, I wasn't discovered until the mid-morning break. Nobody had missed me. This was not a good introduction to the world of learning.

In general, school life settled down and I became a milk monitor. The government paid for every child to have a half pint of milk to be drunk during mid-morning break. When the milk crate arrived the class would line up and it was my job to hand every classmate their bottle.

We had a nit nurse who came to school every month to check our heads for nits in our hair with something like a knitting needle. We all called her Nitty Norah. I joined the school choir run by our headmistress, Miss Greenwood and country dance club run by Miss Barton, who had a famous cousin, *the* Gary Cooper, a film star. After school was always ballet, tap, piano or Girls' Life Brigade (a bit like brownies) run by the Methodist Church.

I was nearly nine years old when disaster struck; It started with a cold that quickly turned into flu, measles and chicken pox, ending up with double pneumonia all because my mother did not believe in vaccinations. When immunisations were given at school my mother overruled my dad and refused to sign the paperwork for authorisation for all the vaccinations other children were quite rightly being given. I became very ill and not responsive to treatment at home so Doctor Thomas, who was a family friend as well as our doctor, called for an ambulance and I was taken, delirious, into the Luton Children's Hospital.

At the beginning I was given forty-eight hours to live but over time I started to recover. One thing I do remember whilst in a semi-conscious state was thinking that every nurse who approached me was my mother and pulling on their uniform, begging to be taken home. I was going to be sent to a convalescent home but they were all full, so I returned to ongoing family care and attended outpatients twice a week back at the hospital to learn how to breathe properly again. Because of this I missed two years' schooling, so I did not take the eleven-plus exam as my headmistress said I had been away from school too long to ever catch up.

Whilst in hospital I struck up a long friendship with a lad called Peter who had dark black hair and a cheeky grin. We were always up to mischief. One day he asked his parents to bring caps into hospital, you know, the type that boys used to put in their toy guns. Anyway, he shared them with me and just as the nurses were coming towards us we used to throw them on the floor so it would make them jump. Naughty, but fun! This idea was fuelled by a hospital visit we had from an actor cowboy called Call McCord who brought his horse with him into the grounds and gave us all a signed photo of them.

When I returned home I spent weekends visiting Grandma and Granddad and one Saturday Granddad gave me a penny (old money) and told me to go down the street to the paper seller to buy a 'green-un'.

Feeling quite grown up I skipped off and upon reaching the paper seller with his old cap on I boldly said as clearly as I could, 'Can I have a green one please?'

'Cor blimey, miss, aren't you posh? Course you can,' replied the paper seller, laughing.

'Thank you,' I replied. On returning to Granddad's shop, I looked at the paper and there printed in black letters on pink paper were the words *'Green-un Sports Paper'*. I did feel daft.

At the age of eleven to thirteen I attended a secondary modern school. The only good things about being there were netball, music and history. Our music teacher, Mr Gallagher, took us to the cinema to see *The Dam Busters* film. He was a very clever man and on return to school he wrote words to the music which accompanied the film but as far as I am aware he never had them published. Maybe I should in his memory. The Suez Canal trouble blew up and we thought we might be at war again, so we all had to learn evacuation procedures.

At thirteen I was sent to a private secretarial school for girls to learn shorthand and typing. Here is where I made friends for life. It was the late fifties by now. I became an avid football supporter of Luton Town FC, skipping lessons to watch their semi-final for the FA Cup.

There were two major plane crashes that devastated us girls – Buddy Holly and the Manchester United team. Now sixteen, we thought our world had come to an end.

A Special Person

Although she began with ten fingers, she didn't keep them all. From the age of five Hepzibah was taught to help her mother in the washroom, particularly with mangling clothes. This was carried out in the wash house which was an outbuilding attached to the cottage. It had two very large sinks, wooden scrubbing boards and of course the mangle, which to me was a lethal weapon. You put clothes in one end in between two large rollers, then you had to turn a handle, the idea being that the rollers would squeeze all the water out of the clothes before you put them on the washing line. Hepzibah grow quite confident with her tasks, but this time was different; she was not concentrating but in a dreamboat kind of mood. She put the garment in the first roller and turned the handle, forgetting to move her hand quick enough, losing the top of her index finger.

Oh God, she thought, but not wanting to appear incompetent she quickly picked the finger up, wiped the blood away, and pushing it back on, wound a cloth around it and carried on as if nothing had happened. Of course, it was crooked all her life. She never complained about it, just told her grandchildren of her many misdemeanours.

Hepzibah Watson, now there is a name to reckon with. A formidable character if ever there was. Born in 1892 with a cheeky smile that stayed with her all her life and deep piercing brown eyes like pools in a lagoon. As a young child her long dark hair was combed into wonderful ringlets by her mother, who twisted her hair round damp rags which in those days had to be slept in because that was the fashion. She wore a pinafore-style dress with long sleeves that she always managed to catch when climbing trees. She was the eldest of three children, having a sister Dorothea who was completely the opposite. Dorothea was a pretty child with blue eyes and the fairest hair you would ever see but very delicate like a flower. Then there was young William who always seemed to be the favourite of their parents and never seemed to do anything wrong.

They lived in Bassingbourn, a small village in the heart of Cambridgeshire. Their Father, William, was a shepherd for the local landowner and squire of the parish up at the big house and their mother Sarah-Anne baked for the local school and took washing in that she did for the villagers. There are so many childhood stories I could tell of Granny growing up. This one, I think, is my favourite as she was often seen with her dolls' pram full of produce she had picked from the villagers' allotments heading across the fields to Royston Market. I think they got so used to her everyone turned a blind eye, including the local policeman. Another is when her mother had just done a particularly large bake for the local school and Hepzibah thought it quite funny to tie her siblings' legs to the wooden kitchen table so that when they stood up the table shook and all the hard work of her mum fell to the floor. Then there was the night she put a frog in her parents' bed just to give them a scare.

Then of course there was maiden Aunt Clara, poor simple Clara. Clara was feeling miserable with a dreadful cold that confined her to bed with a runny, sore red nose. Hepzibah, now age ten, came to the rescue and knitted her aunt a nose bag and yes it was worn proudly by Clara.

However, leaving the village school at the age of fourteen she was thrust into domestic life which I can honestly say was the making of her. It brought discipline and structure to her otherwise chaotic tomboy lifestyle. Her first position was with a family of milliners in Luton in the county of Bedfordshire as a junior house maid.

She was sixteen when Granddad came into her life. They met at a village dance, but Victor Percy was about to be sent to London to train as an apprentice shoe-maker, boot-maker and repairer. He was tall, dark and although he walked with a limp sustained from a childhood illness, he caused quite a stir with the village lasses. He was four years older than Granny.

Granddad's apprenticeship took him to Edmonton, London. He lodged in South Street and Granny shortly followed him, obtaining a position as a lady's maid living in North Street and, believe it or not, the back yards to these properties literally backed on to each other. Time moved on and at the age of nineteen Granny found herself pregnant with her first child. Hepzibah and Victor married at Edmonton Registry Office when she was six months' pregnant. their ages being nineteen and twenty-three. In those days if you were under the age of twenty-one you would have to get permission from your father to marry. To get round this looming problem Granny simply told a lie, declaring to the registrar that her father was dead so he could not be a witness. No, he was very much alive, proven by family documents of a later date.

Granddad was offered a position with a cobbler in Dunstable in Bedfordshire, but now with a wife and child in tow he needed accommodation. As luck would have it this offer came with accommodation above the cobbler's shop. All was well, child number two and three came along, World War One came and went. It was World War Two that really shaped Hepzibah's life. To my way of thinking this is where my gran came into her own, for her cheeky determination stood her in good stead because she never took no for an answer. It just wasn't in her vocabulary. She became a member of the Women's Royal Voluntary Service and was put in charge of the whole evacuee situation for Bedfordshire. Refugees were put on a train in London and sent to Bedfordshire, where Granny delegated homes for them with local families. She dealt with all their personal problems, ran soup kitchens, distributed clothing and was literally in her element, for she had found something she was really good at, organizing.

During World War Two an organization was formed to help raise money for ambulances. Families paid just one penny a week to help raise this money. Hepzibah collected this on behalf of the Red Cross and was sent a letter from the Duke of Gloucester thanking her for her war efforts.

Growing up with this incredible lady in my life taught me a lot. After the war she used to take me with her to the Conservative offices, where she organized meetings and afternoon teas. Her main job was manager of a cake shop in the centre of town which became my second home. She organized monthly coach trips for businesspeople of the town, either to London to see a show, or a boat trip on the River Thames down to Margate. Oh! The knitting of endless grey socks when I would have to hold the wool in both hands whilst she wound it into a ball. We went on weekend picnics when Granddad would just stop the car at the side of the road, get out the picnic basket, the kettle and light the gas can for tea.

These were wonderful carefree days. I learnt a lot from my gran, Hepzibah. Her motto was 'I can and I will' and this has always carried me through my life too.

An Unusual Holiday

Armed with a rifle, the German guard signalled to us to get out of our car. My heart was racing as my Dutch friend told me to do exactly as he had asked, but slowly and as I did, she whispered, 'Don't you say a word, leave all the talking to me as he will immediately realize you are English and that may antagonise him.' He approached us quite menacingly and proceeded to search our car.

A second guard then appeared, beckoning us into what I can only describe as a small garden shed. Once inside he took our passports and gestured to me to give him my camera which he then proceeded to dismantle. I was a mere twenty-one years of age so this whole experience was alien to me, not at all what I had been used to back home in England. Our handbags were searched; this made me feel very uncomfortable, an invasion of privacy. I could feel the palms of my hands becoming wet and clammy. I wondered what would be next and could not wait to get away from there. The guards were laughing and seemed to be sharing a private joke which I thought was extremely rude behaviour. After what seemed to be a lifetime the barrier was finally lifted and we were allowed into Germany.

This was post-war Germany and my eyes could not believe what they were seeing; it was such a stark contrast to the Holland I had just left. Woman were tending fields with old-fashioned equipment. They didn't smile or look up and wore long drab clothing with scarves tied around their heads. An unexpected sight that will stay with me forever. We had lunch in a nearby town and did a little exploring before returning to that border crossing which I was so dreading.

It was early evening, the sun had started to go down but I was so grateful to be going back into Holland. Returning was not so scary since the guards lifted the barrier and let us straight through. I breathed a huge sigh of relief. When we got home it was explained to me that there was still a lot of smuggling going on between the countries in such things as butter, cheese and so on.

I had travelled to Holland to visit a friend, and this was my first holiday on my own. My friend Fieneke was a dental student and lived in a flat in Rotterdam. She met me at the airport, then explained she had to work that week and I was to be put on a train to stay with her parents and two brothers in the north of Holland to spend my first week.

After a two-hour journey I arrived at Bellingwolde station to be met by Mr and Mrs Georgen who spoke very little English and I knew nothing about the Dutch language. I was greeted warmly with just one question, 'What did your father do in the war?' I managed to explain with hand gestures that Dad repaired damaged fighter and bomber planes so they could return to service.

My hosts lived on the outskirts of the village in a lovely old farmhouse with their two sons Han and Johan. Our first meal together was with a dictionary between us; I had to try Dutch and they would try English which caused a lot of laughter.

The cellar of my hosts' farmhouse held a few secrets of its own. I remember the walls were painted white and the family's clogs stood in a corner like soldiers on parade. I was then told some wonderful heroic stories from World War Two of an airman being shot down and hidden within the walls of this great building. 'Try and find the hiding holes,' Mr Georgan said, 'go on, try.' I walked round without a single clue. The bricks were laid in a sequence and if you pushed the right brick the wall would give up its secret. Hidden passages which if followed would lead you way out into the surrounding fields, well away from the village before surfacing, hopefully safely. They had to be extremely careful as the German border was just four kilometres away.

On the fourth day of my stay, I was woken up but a very loud bang on the front door. I could hear raised voices and crying coming from outside. What on earth has happened? I thought. Then the local postman came into the house; he was banging his fists on the table telling us that the German border guards had shot their much-loved local vicar. He had been hit in the back of the neck and died instantly. Apparently, the guards said they thought he was smuggling as he had not stopped at the border as he usually did.

A wave of disbelief and bewilderment ran through the village. The villagers began to talk. Was war starting all over again? They could simply not repeat that tyranny. The local garage proprietor later found that the brakes on the vicar's car had failed and he had no choice, there was no way he could stop his car. It seemed I had stumbled into a very different, scary world. Could anyone be trusted? Was this a fault of the car? Or had his brakes been cut? There seemed to be a suspicion. My mind was working overtime. I felt I had been transported into a fiction novel.

The following day I was sent to the butcher's so off I trotted with my basket and shopping list clutched tightly in my hand. Down the pretty tree-lined main street thoughts were going through my mind: They won't understand me ... I am English, they are Dutch ...

Opening the door, I cautiously walked into the shop as a bell rang gently above me. I could feel eyes piercing into my skin from all angles as suddenly I became the centre of attention. I could believe I could hear their minds ticking over; who was this English stranger? Now inside the shop, I tried to very slowly ask for some sausages, when to my amazement a London accent greeted me with, 'What part of Blighty are you from then, me dear?' I was astounded, the Butcher was English, so the joke was on me. He told me that half the villagers were either ex-RAF or army soldiers that came back after the war to marry their Dutch sweethearts. It was wonderful so many questions were being thrown at me. I found my confidence to speak to anyone in the village that passed me. The Dutch are very polite, the men touch their caps, the ladies smile and nod. A very friendly country indeed.

The end of my first week in Holland was over much too soon and Fieneke arrived to take me back to the big city of Rotterdam to her flat on the top floor. They have a great idea with flats as they all look after each other. On the ground floor are the older people, on the next floor a family, with the top floor for single, younger people. It is a formula that could work anywhere in the world. Every day they check on each other to see if everyone is well or if the older people need shopping. Or even just to say a friendly hello.

I spent the next two weeks touring Amsterdam, Eindhoven, Essen and of course Rotterdam. It was a wonderful experience.

Mike Reeves

Mike Reeves   Where I'm From

I'm from a time when I just had my mother,
No sister or brother, we just had each other.

I'm from a time when our dads were away,
Defending our freedom and saving the day.

I'm from an era of respect, love and caring,
A mother who taught me to focus on sharing.

I'm from a childhood so rich in joy,
I sometimes wish I was still a boy.

I'm from a time I will always treasure,
Work, love and memories all beyond measure.

I'm from these years when time moves so fast,
I wish it would simply slow down and last.

My grandchildren make me so happy and proud,
Working, studying, staying safe in a crowd.

I'm in a pandemic, shielding my life,
Hoping that Science will erase the strife.

Beginnings

I held the flickering candle as I peered out of the window at my mother's retreating figure. She had gone to the grocer's shop at the corner of Guildford Street to get change for the gas meter. We had no electricity in our house, just gas. I leant a little closer to the window, watching eagerly for her return. Before I knew it flames were leaping up the curtains.

All of sudden, Mr Short, from number 16, ran into our house, picked me up and rushed me to the front door. He ripped down the net curtains and trampled out the fire I had started with the candle.

The next day we travelled to Tealby for our Christmas holiday, and our near disaster was relayed to all the family. The good thing was, I was spoilt regarding pocket money and Christmas presents. I enjoyed all the sweets and listening to the radio with my grandmother, also a HMV gramophone as it was known as in those days. This is when I started to enjoy dance-band music, even at that age. Famous dance bands such as Bert Ambrose, Roy Fox and Glen Miller, and not to mention artists like Al Bowlly, Vera Lynn, Doris Day and Frank Sinatra. When Christmas was over, it was time to return to Grimsby, with no road closures. I was hoping the B1203 at Bully Hill might be blocked so we would have to stay in Tealby until the bad weather had gone.

Delays were typical. The next holiday we had there the coach broke down at Binbrook. Luckily, the landlord at the Marquis of

Granby public house allowed my mother to ring Tealby Post Office and I presumed Mr Lee the postmaster alerted my grandmother to our delay. I remember having a lovely cream tea and a ride on my newly painted black tricycle when we arrived later that day.

During that week the village had a carnival in the grounds of Bayon's Manor. During WWII the manor was used by the British Army. My grandmother told me the famous Tennyson family owned this wonderful stately home. Unfortunately, in the mid-sixties, it was demolished.

There were mishaps too. On another occasion, I remember looking out of my bedroom window and seeing that the milkman had delivered a jug of milk to the front door. Watching the horse-drawn cart, and it carrying a milk churn, amazed me so I ran downstairs, knocking over the jug of milk. Uncle Jim had to run after the milkman to replace it.

The holiday seemed to go on forever during this summer break. As the weeks rolled by different aunts and uncles arrived at number 29 Front Street and gave me pocket money for my summer holidays. I think you could say I was spoilt.

The River Rase was at the bottom of Front Street, just past the King's Head public house. I spent many hours with my jam jar secured with string around the collar to carry it when filled with water. My home-made fishing net consisting of a bamboo cane and a wire coat hanger to form a ring was secured to the cane, with an old onion bag fixed to the ring with string. Now I just had to catch the tadpoles. The water only came up to my ankles and it was easy to step out of the river. Also, other children and parents were standing very close. I enjoyed many happy days that summer.

Years later, whenever I bought a new car in August, I would take my family to Tealby to the King's Head and think of my childhood holidays in this lovely, award-winning village.

School Days

Back home in Grimsby, I can just remember the corrugated Anderson air raid shelters, on the bombed area close to my home, 20 Guildford Street. The shelters remained in situ for many months after the war ended, and we played inside them. The council eventually removed these shelters in preparation for the foundations for the erection of four council houses to replace the bombed terraced houses.

The dug-out foundation trenches became an ideal play area for our war games. My pal, Malcolm Woods, provided our Union Jack fixed to a broom handle. We played for hours at these war games in the trenches. The building site progressed, and a watchman was employed as building materials had arrived on site and this was the end of our trench games. During the war effort iron railings had been removed from pathways, often leaving 5mm metal above the pathway slab. As I ran during another war game I tripped with the Union Jack, not seeing the metal, and the metal cut open my leg. I finished up at the Grimsby General Hospital. I can still remember the pain from the stitches as no local anaesthetic was given. I still have the scar.

Many years later, in the 1960s, as an apprentice electrician working in a display window, I tripped and fell through the glass, so now I have a scar on both legs, although this time I did have an anaesthetic.

In February 1948 I remember playing on the area now cleared of four bombed dwellings. As I played with this old piano dumped near Hilda Street School, I could see beyond the school gates children in lines waiting to go into their classrooms. I thought, soon I'll be joining those lines.

The first day I started school I walked into this large hall and on the middle of the floor lay a large sandpit. I thought this was far better than the bombed site where my friends and I used for play. At twelve noon I walked home for my dinner, thinking school had finished for the day, only to be told by my mother I had to be back at school after my dinner.

I remember being sad and scared during my early school days. Miss Bean, the teacher, insisted I didn't write with my left hand which she would slap with a rule. In those days we had an inkwell and pen so when we tried to write with our left hand you smudged your writing which she showed to the class. When I look back, I wonder why the teachers didn't let left-handed children use pencils? I wasn't on my own; several other left-handed children also experienced the pain I went through.

This trauma continued during our early days at school. I would make excuses to my mother that I wasn't feeling well, hoping I could take the day off. Then I caught the measles, not realising how ill I was. It seemed wonderful with all the visitors I received and not having to write.

When I returned to school I had been moved to the back of the classroom; this is when I told the teacher the writing on the blackboard was obscured. A visit to Burgess Street eye clinic resulted in my having to wear these dreadful tortoiseshell glasses complete with the teasing. Returning to school, and when I look back in time, this is why I found the classroom an alien place to be. Not only was I left-handed, I also struggled to see the blackboard.

We now moved on to primary school. Mr Jones was a good teacher. I enjoyed his teaching and progress was made. Thanks to Mr Jones I learnt to write curving my left hand.

I caught German measles which seemed to affect my eyesight, and the room had to be darkened longer than when I had the measles. However, eventually, I returned to Mr Jones and his fine teaching, especially his maths, although I had missed some lessons.

Then we moved to my next form with Mr Aitken. On my first day I asked Mr Aitken if I could move to the front of the class as I was sat on the back row and had difficulty seeing the blackboard. He allowed me to move. 'I seemed to have difficulty reading some of the words on the blackboard,' I explained.

He then said I was a desiccated lump of cheese. The classroom laughed, he laughed, I felt stupid.

The next day in the playground the bully of our school called me a cheesecake and punched me. My uncle Fred had told me if ever you get bullied at school, just punch them on the nose. So, I did. Blood covered his shirt and he started to cry. The playground teacher sent me to the headteacher, Mr White, and I was caned. I felt guilty having given this bully a heavy nosebleed.

The humiliations from this teacher would soon be over as I would be moving to Mr Lincoln's class. He was like Mr Jones and I enjoyed every moment in this class. We learnt new skills in craft, art and maths, and I even liked the English lessons. On meeting Mr Lincoln many years later, I told him how much I had enjoyed his and Mr Jones's classes. It seems to me some teachers are better at recognising students' fears and anxieties than others.

When I moved to the secondary school I discovered I was dyslexic, yet I gradually made progress in my learning because all the teachers in this school taught me well. I enjoyed science with Mr Fretwell; the magnetism fascinated me and the maths too. Mr Cressey's metalwork classes gave me skills I would find useful later in my working life.

However, it was the library books on science, especially magnetism and electricity, that led to my yearning for a career in that field. I loved the craft and metalwork classes at which I excelled. In fact, on the last school open day, I had made many of the craft exhibits on display including a wrought-iron table lamp. The shade was constructed from pleated patterned paper mounted on a copper-wired frame. Sadly, none of my family were able to attend.

I worked hard in all the school subjects and improved in exam results. I came second in the class in my final year and received a book prize for progress in my education: *Electrical Installation Work*. When the careers' teacher asked what career I hoped to pursue, I replied that I wanted to become an electrician. He swiftly replied, 'No, no you're not capable of doing that. A big lad like you will make a good barrow boy on the pontoon down on the docks and earn a good wage.'

Many years later I remember designing the electrical rewire of the careers' office. This involved the preparation of drawings and specification of the proposed electrical installation. During the first pre-start meeting I met the same careers' officer who may have persuaded me take up a different career.

In 1958, at fifteen years old, I started work in a sawmill as a labourer. I asked the manager if I could attend the College of Further Education on Fridays without pay. He agreed, provided I did four hours' work on a Saturday morning, which I accepted.

Once again, I had a very good teacher, Mr Evans, which was lucky as I found maths hard. He taught me how to use a slide rule which made the calculations quicker than log tables, especially in examinations when time was important for each question.

Well, the following June arrived. I sat the exam and I sensed the anxiety around me, as did my student friends. On receiving my pass results I trawled the town visiting every electrical contractor, applying for the position as an apprentice electrician.

At the interview I stated I had passed the first year in electrical installation work. The next week a letter arrived stating I had to start in two weeks' time, just enough time to hand in my notice at the sawmill.

After four years at the college I gained all my City & Guilds Certificates and before the end of the decade I had my own electrical contracting company.

On reflection, being left-handed, wearing glasses and being dyslexic wasn't a good start in my early education in the late forties and early fifties. I often wonder how those other children going through the same fear and anxiety as I did in those days are doing today.

A Journey through My Working Life

On Fridays I attended Grimsby College on day release in electrical installation work. My first working week comprised electrical maintenance on steam trawler. I remember being scared climbing the mast to carry out repairs on the steaming, fishing and all-round lights. In those days no provisions for a safety harness existed. Luckily, in my school days many of us did climb trees, so mast climbing on the trawlers didn't present a problem for me.

However, on one occasion the mast headlight lamp failed, and I was sent out into the estuary via a tug to replace the lamp. I found climbing the mast quite scary as fierce waves dashed against the boat, but I succeeded in replacing the spent lamp. I think working up the mast while the trawlers berthed at the coal hoist gave me confidence in working in the estuary. The coal hoist is no longer in existence. It used to load coal into the steam trawlers prior to the next trip to the fishing grounds. Often in windy weather coal dust became a hazardous situation while working up the mast. In those days we worked most bank holidays if required to ensure there were no delays in sailing.

On another working day I was sent to New Waltham Royal Navy Wireless Station, working in the stand by the generator room. The station had four masts and red warning lights for low-flying aircraft. An electrician came from Sheffield to do routine maintenance and replace the lamps serving the warning lights. I was so pleased that was not a duty I had to perform.

My next experience involved travelling to Blackburn Aircraft at Brough, East Yorkshire. I left my home at 6 a.m. and walked to Railway Street in Grimsby, arriving at the dock station. I caught the train to New Holland and then took the *Lincoln Castle* paddle steamer to Hull. From Wellington Street I took a bus to Hull Paragon Railway Station, next by train again to Brough. I finally arrived at my place of work, after a short walk from the station. My first duty was making the drinks for the electricians at tea break. After the break we walked through hangers to carry out our electrical installation work.

While walking through the hangers I was amazed at the size of the Blackburn Beverly freighter, a huge vehicle and troop carrier stationed at Abingdon in Oxfordshire which could carry thirty paratroopers, land on sand and even reverse. I saw too the Blackburn Buccaneer (Admiralty ref; NA 39) I've remembered that reference all my working life. The Buccaneer nuclear bomber began service in the Royal Navy in 1962. This swing-winged aircraft was designed to serve on aircraft carriers and could fly at low altitude to avoid radar detection. I lodged in Northfield Road Hull, Monday to Wednesday, then came home on Thursday evening via the same transport to attend Grimsby College on Fridays.

I finally returned home to complete my apprenticeship at the Grimsby College of Technology, having gained contracts rewiring electrical installations in our local schools and food factories. I was very fortunate to be trained by excellent technical electricians and lecturers.

On completion of my apprenticeship, I wanted to gain experience in other types of electrical installation work, for example building electrical control panels to serve, swimming pools, ice rinks, boiler houses for heating systems and engine rooms for refrigeration plants. So, I went back to Grimsby College and gained additional qualifications in controls. Then I applied for the position as an electrical technician with an international refrigeration company, commissioning control panels serving the refrigeration plants. Having spent time working away from home in Cork, Dublin, Belfast, Aberdeen and Dundee.

I came home and decided it was time to start up an electrical contracting business. Whilst I enjoyed this, I continued to carry out the electrical installation work, rather than the office side of the business. I had two partners, one of whom carried out the process of obtaining the work via tenders. I gained many skills during this period of my working life, replacing the existing electrical installations in schools, hospitals, public and commercial buildings. I still had the desire to build the control panels I had maintained in my early days while working away.

The opportunity arose for me to start building these control panels, which I did. I found this type of electrical work the most rewarding throughout my working life. I didn't want to just build these control panels, I wanted to design, provide schematic drawings, tender for the work, on completion install and commission the controls for the proposed plant. This I succeeded in doing.

Due to unforeseen circumstances, I took a position as an engineering surveyor with the then County Council and was responsible for all electrical and mechanical installations at the Grimsby College, schools and public buildings. I made this move because my wife became ill with multiple sclerosis, and it was easier to get home at lunchtime to see her.

In 1995 I took early retirement and became a carer to care for my disabled wife. With support from our Social Services, medical practice and the NHS, I continued with my caring role until, sadly, my wife died.

Throughout my working life I have been so grateful for those patient teachers and lecturers who educated me and helped me to realise that I am of value. Despite being retired for the last twenty-five years, I still miss the buzz of resolving engineering defects.

A Special Person

The sirens sound and the bombs fall, numbers 24 to 30 Guildford Street are destroyed; I am at number 20 in the cupboard under the stairs. Cradled and shielded by my mother and told to be brave, everything will be OK. I think the dreadful gas mask scared me more than the bombs exploding. I have memories of incendiary bombs lighting up the street and the smell of dust. Later, carbolic soap when the inside of our house had been cleaned. We all loved our mothers, and we were all totally reliant on them during the war years, while our fathers were away defending our freedom.

Like many children after the war being brought up by our mothers I remember, in a typical day, the mornings sitting, watching her scrubbing the bar floors at the Imperial Hotel, Grimsby Road, Cleethorpes. Then returning home and getting me ready for school, after which she would return to Cleethorpes, to work in Wonderland as a cashier. Often when off school I would play on the sand by myself and run into Wonderland to tell Mother I was OK. We spent time together during and after tea. During Friday and Saturday evenings she would work at the Imperial Hotel as a barmaid. I would be cared for by a neighbour, who Mother would pay.

We would look forward to Fridays as pay day allowed us to shop for pork, fruit and sweets. Although ration books determined the food available, we enjoyed certain food for three days. Monday to Thursday we had make do for meals, depending on what was remaining from the weekend. Failing that, we could buy food on the tick from the Waverley corner cake shop, then pay the bill on a Friday. At a very early age I became capable of making myself scrambled egg or beans on toast during school holidays while Mother worked.

I remember being sent to the fruit shop in Oxford Street and Mother said only ask the nice lady if we could have some potatoes on the tick, but the other lady tried to serve me instead. I said to her, 'I want to be served by the nice lady,' to which she replied, 'Am I not a nice lady?' Needless to say, I was never sent to the fruit shop again. At the end of summer free food became available in the hedgerows, with brambles and ground-fall apples in abundance.

For reasons I don't know Mother became housekeeper for a couple. The wife of the couple was disabled, the husband was a doctor. This made life easier for Mother only having one job and we spent more time together which I enjoyed. We returned home daily.

Mother became ill and was sent to Springfield isolation hospital with a lung infection. My aunt came to look after me during the isolation period. I cycled to the isolation ward in Springfield Road asking a passer-by for directions, hoping to see my mother, only to be told this visit had be done through the small window in her isolation bedroom door. I remember feeling so sad not holding her hand. This has been relived to me during the recent pandemic, when families have to visit their loved ones through a screen. It seemed a lifetime waiting for her to come home. But the day did arrive, and I was so pleased to see that ambulance returning Mother.

Several days later we walked up Hainton Avenue and turned right into Welholme Road adjacent to the railway crossing. We entered this large house, known as Corby House. I remember coming out with a ten-shilling note. We had no money as Mother had been ill. I suppose this would have been a benefit payment.

Mother taught me how to wallpaper and cut straight; we had to cut one side of the wallpaper before the pasting, that was my job. I was also taught to apply distemper to the walls and ceiling. This was like the emulsion we would use today. Another duty I had involved a wheelbarrow and a long walk to Catherine Street Gas Works to bring back bags of coke for the fire. On my return the fire grate had been spruced up with a coat of black lead.

During my last year at school I began working for a grocer's in Kent Street as an errand boy delivering groceries around the town. My carrier bike became quite useful during school gardening days in Ladysmith Road, as often I was asked to bring vegetables back to the school. When I got paid, I would buy groceries from my place of work with a discount as I wanted to help Mother with the bills.

Not long after leaving school and starting work we knocked down the pantry together and employed a plasterer to make good the walls. We then mounted a Belfast sink in the space of the old pantry. We plumbed in a cold-water tap and a waste pipe to the outside drain.

Mother became a waitress which she enjoyed, working at the Royal Hotel, Talk of the Town and the Winter Gardens. But what I mostly remember was when she became a silver service waitress at the Kingsway Hotel she would use Robin starch for her apron, black skirt, blouse and shoes which had to be immaculate. It was a joy to see how happy she became working at this splendid hotel.

This is the lady I want to focus on, who brought me up to be brave, strong through sickness and in health and to work hard. Thanks to my mother, she taught me not to be selfish, but to be loving, caring, respectful to others and who I am today. I can truly say when Mother died I lost my best friend. I spent many hours on my own as a child while Mother worked; now in old age I cope very well being on my own in isolation while shielding, it's as if history is repeating itself, sadly, without my mother.

However, we are now free of lockdown and I can't wait to meet the friends I have made at Friends at Home face to face at local venues. Even, one day, meeting the friends I have made at *My Mother's Purse*, not forgetting Mary, my telephone friend.

Jackie Kirk

Jackie Kirk Where I'm From

I come from Grimsby
It makes you think of fish

The smell of the Pyewipe factory
The fish products made for pet food
Was the aroma of my childhood
Pervading everywhere we went

I am from my dad
He was a railway man
Standing on the footplate
Shovelling coal into the furnace
Turning inky black with dirt

I come from Grimsby
It makes you think of fish

My family didn't go to sea
Apart from Grandad Tom
He was a trawler mate
A long, long time ago

The trawlers are all gone now
The docks so empty and different
Will they get a new life?
It's very hard to know

I come from Grimsby
It makes you think of fish

Beginnings

I was born in August in 1946, the year after the end of World War Two. It seems we lived in rooms at first. It was common at that time for people to rent out a part of their home. One family lived in half the house and another family in the other half. My mum told me that we lived in Cleethorpes at that time, and she took me for walks along the front in my pram.

Next, we lived with my dad's parents in Freshney Street. It no longer exists and became Freshney Drive when a lot of houses were demolished in the 1970s. The Grimsby hospital and nurses' home were nearby and were also demolished at that time and Waterside Drive was built. I don't know what we did for a hospital then as the present one was not opened until 1983.

Granny and Grandad's house was straight onto the street with no front garden. It had a long back garden where they grew fruit and vegetables. They had a beautiful lilac tree and whenever I see one it reminds me of them. The toilet was in the back garden and before we lived there, Grandad kept rabbits, with which he sometimes won prizes in shows. While living there I went to the nursery at South Parade School. In the afternoons we had a lie down and my bed had a picture of a clock on it.

After a while we moved to rent rooms at the back of a shop on Oliver Street which fronted onto Ayscough Street, another one no longer there. I don't know if it is my memory, or I was told it, but I was in a cot looking up at the light which was covered as I had measles. I played with two girls who lived in Freshney Street. Anne Clayton had dark hair and pigtails. Lesley Dimbleby had fair hair and wore glasses. I can't remember what we played.

When I was nearly six, we moved to a rented house in Cleveland Street, which is at the bottom of Cleveland Bridge. The traffic used to drive over the bridge in those days. We called it The Tip and it seems there had been a rubbish tip on the other side of the bridge at one time. The house fronts straight onto the street and has a concrete backyard. I can remember going with my parents to look at the house before they took it on, but all I remember is a big dog and a toddler sitting on a potty in the backyard. The toilet was in the yard and also a coal house where coal was stored for the open fire in the living room. When we moved our furniture came in a big removal van. As an only child I was lucky to have quite a lot of toys. Most families at that time usually had around six children. My friends later told me that they thought I was posh because I had a wooden desk and chair to play with.

I'll tell you a bit about my neighbourhood. At the back of the houses on our street there was a passage with a wire fence onto a field. We always called it the cow field and I later found it was owned by a farmer named Stones. Years before there had been greyhound racing on that field. We could still see remnants of the concrete track when we played there. Down the side passage were the back gardens of the houses that front onto Gilbey Road. I can't remember them all, but the first one, the backyard of the shop on the corner. That was run by a Mrs Welbourne. My mother worked there at one time. Next door was my mother's friend Vera, and Arthur. I always called her Aunty Vera, even though she was no relation.

Further along the passage was the Avison family. They had two boys, Steven and Paul. The Avisons had a twelve-inch black-and-white television, which none of the neighbours had at that time.

Lots of us crowded into their house to watch the Queen's Coronation in 1953. I remember we were given a blue book with a coin in it at school.

At the end of the block was Mr Douglas, who had a hardware shop in Corporation Road. My cousins Peter and Lesley, who is the same age as Margaret, lived nearby in New Haven Terrace. Peter, two years older, has now passed away. I played with Lesley, Margaret and the Avison boys at times, apart from Steven, who became a local councillor in later years.

Sometimes we played in the street. We played marbles in the drain covers and two balls up the wall or whip and top. We always coloured our tops with chalk, making patterns. In good weather we played in the field. At the back of the field are railway lines which run under Cleveland Bridge. The side of the bridge is grass covered and we played along its sides. Once I picked some flowers and took them home to my mother. She wasn't particularly happy and called them weeds. I found out in later years that they were wildflowers that often grow at the side of railway lines and are called rose bay willow herb.

That wasn't the only time my good deed went awry. In another memory I got up before my parents one Mother's Day. I decided to light the coal fire for my mother as a present. With a coal fire we used to hold newspaper up in front of it to draw the flames up the chimney. I don't know what happened, but I dropped the paper, and it burned the rug in front of the fire. That didn't turn out to be a particularly good present!

School Days

I started at South Parade Nursery in around 1949. All I can remember is that the teacher was Miss Milton and she looked old with grey hair in a bun. I wonder how old she actually was. We had a lie down in the afternoons and my bed had a picture of a clock on it.

When I was nearly six, we moved house and I started in the infants at Littlecoates Primary School. Both my mother and two of my aunts had attended there in years gone by. Our house was in the street next to the school, so my mother used to lift me over the wall into the playground so that I didn't have to go round the block to the gate. I can only remember the headmistress, Miss Nicholson. We went into the hall each morning and she would be on the stage. I remember a boy called Keith Goodman. I don't know what he had done wrong, but he was called out onto the stage in front of everyone, put over Miss Nicholson's knee and she smacked him with a slipper.

At the age of seven I moved into the juniors. Naughty boys and girls would get the cane, but I don't really know what they had done as, thankfully, it never happened to me. I stayed for school dinners as my mother worked. I loved all the meals. They were mostly meat, potatoes and vegetables, but the puddings were the best. I especially liked chocolate concrete and chocolate custard. Cornflake tart and custard was another favourite, so crunchy. The dinner hall was a detached building on the edge of the field. I remember once leaving after dinner and passing a little girl sat at the table crying. The dinner lady was standing behind her and saying, 'You will sit there until you have eaten it all.'

From Years 2 to 4 I remember my teachers were ginger-haired Mrs Pett; Mr Graham, who was tall and slim and wore a suit; Miss Elliot, who wasn't very tall and had a wrinkly face, but was very sporty. We played netball in the playground with her. I wasn't particularly good and hated it.

During that final fourth year, the headmaster, Mr Broxom, retired. I was chosen to present his retirement present. During playtime we often used to play on the cross. It was in the corner of the playground and was obviously a war memorial, though we didn't realise it at the time. In later years it was moved outside of the playground which was a good idea.

In that fourth year we took the eleven-plus exam. There were three tiers. The best pupils passed to go to Wintringham Grammar School. The next tier, which I passed for, was Grimsby Technical Secondary School. The building is still there in Eleanor Street but is incredibly sad to see, as it is a listed building and has gone to ruin. Those who didn't pass the eleven-plus went to Armstrong Secondary School, off Corporation Road. It had to be demolished in later years as it was marshland, and the building was starting to sink down. A community centre is now on part of the land.

So, in the September of 1957 I started at Grimsby Technical Secondary School. We had to wear a uniform to school, which was bottle green, with a white blouse, a tie and grey skirt, along with a bottle-green blazer. Girls wore bottle-green knickers for PE. I can remember having to climb up wall bars and trying to climb up a rope. I could never manage the rope. I was lucky to get a new uniform each year. I can remember a girl in the year above me who wore a very faded blazer. I knew her in later years and found out that she came from a very big family.

My first friend there was Sandra Sorley, who lived not far from me. We went on the bus to school. The school times were different then and we started at 9.15 in the morning until 4.15 in the afternoon. We had an hour and a half for lunch. My mother gave me money for my dinner. Often Sandra and I would walk down Freeman Street and go in a café on Cleethorpes Road that had a jukebox playing the latest records. The café was on the second block from Riby Square. It was the late 1950s and I liked Elvis Presley a lot. I had posters of him on my bedroom wall at home. All the latest songs were on the jukebox.

Another friend then was Jose Dowle. She lived on the Nunsthorpe estate and had several brothers and sisters. She sometimes came home with me, and we played in my bedroom with my dolls and my desk and chair. We also played music on my record player. When Jose left school at sixteen, she went to be a nursery nurse in York. She married there and never came back to Grimsby. We still keep in touch regularly. My other friend was Kathleen Lowther. She lived on Hainton Avenue and had a lot of brothers and sisters. Her mother was a lot older than mine and had white hair. I sometimes went to a youth club with her at a church hall on Heneage Road. There was a DJ, and the latest records of the day were played. I met my first boyfriend there. Kath was bridesmaid when I married in 1963, aged seventeen.

I remember some of my teachers. Our French teacher, Miss Fowler, had a wooden leg, so limped slightly. She later married one of the other teachers. Our music teacher was Mr Solomon, who became well known in the town in The Leo Solomon Trio, playing jazz music. I loved music and singing. He became our form teacher in one of the years. I liked him the best of my teachers. He was firm but fair and the music lessons were my favourite. I learned a lot from him. We had Miss Curley for religious instruction. She was form teacher to girls two years older than us and I remember it was a scandal at the time that one of her girls had to leave school because she was having a baby. Our economics teacher was Mr Higson. If he wasn't happy with someone, he would throw the board rubber at them! I liked lessons but hated exams so didn't do particularly well and only passed three 'O' Levels.

Career and Marriage

I left school in July 1962 as I turned sixteen in the August of that year. My first job was at Peter Dixon's Paper Mill in Pyewipe Road, not far away from my home. My knees were knocking and my palms sweating as I arrived for my first day, a little overwhelmed. I worked in the laboratory and titrated liquids used in the paper production. On one day someone spilled acid onto the floor and the office lady slipped and fell in it. She was quite badly burned and had to be off work.

I was then moved into the darkroom. My boss was taking photographs of houses in Stortford Street that were being demolished for an extension to the factory. I enjoyed working in there on my own.

At that time, I sang in the local church choir and met Bill Bradley, who was an altar server. I fancied him because of the white mackintosh that he wore. After a while we wanted to get engaged but my parents said no. Bill was a member of the Church Lads' Brigade and played a drum. I became pregnant and it was the custom at that time to get married as soon as possible. My dad offered us either a white wedding dress or £50 deposit on the house we had found. I sometimes wish I had the wedding dress, but a house was much more practical.

It was a terraced house within a short distance from both my parents and Bill's parents. I found a lovely brown suit and shoes for my November 1963 wedding. I had wanted a lemon pillbox hat like Jackie Kennedy wore but couldn't find one at that time of year so had to make do with a light brown one. My sister was aged four at the time, so my dad carried her. I think my mother was still upset about me getting pregnant. In hindsight I now know why. I found out this year that she was unmarried and had a baby adopted. I now have an older sister who shares the same first name as me.

My husband Bill came from a big family, and they all came to the wedding. Apart from a new bed, our furniture was either donated or second-hand as we didn't have any savings. As I had been an only one until aged thirteen and was never made to do chores, I didn't know much at all about running a house.

My first Christmas in the house was eventful. We had a chicken, but it turned out I had put stuffing into the neck of it instead of the other end. The gas pressure in the cooker dropped so the chicken wasn't cooking very quickly at all. We took it to my mother-in-law's and finished the cooking there, so it was teatime when we finally had our Christmas lunch. This wasn't my only culinary disaster. Years later, my husband bought me a microwave oven. I didn't know much about them and cooked sausages. They looked lovely but when I cut into them, they were charred solid inside. For all the years after during the twenty years I was married to Bill, we went to my parents' house for Christmas dinner.

My daughter was born in June 1964. I was booked to go into Croft Baker maternity home, but she was three weeks late, so I was moved to Nunsthorpe maternity home. I understand that ladies are not left to go so long over their due date now. It just shows how times have changed when I tell you that when the registrar came to the home to register her birth, I wanted to call her Michele (one L). He said, 'That isn't allowed, you have to have two letter "L"s, so she is called Michelle.' I am reminded of that every time I see what some people call their children nowadays.

I had learned to knit while pregnant and so had been knitting a baby jacket. It took me quite a while. It became greyer and greyer by the time I had finished it, so I decided to put it into the copper tub we had for washing clothes to get it white again. I obviously had the water temperature too high as it would have fitted a child's doll by the time it came out. It was another learning curve for me.

It was an old house and we kept dirty washing in a dolly tub under the stairs. One day when I was pulling out the washing there was a clang against the side of the tub. It was a dead rat. I screamed and shoved all the washing back in for Bill to sort it out. We had a kitchen cabinet for food. There were no fitted cupboards in those years. I used to keep boxes of cereal on top of it and I think that was what the rat fed on. Thankfully Bill got rid of it and I never saw one again.

Bill worked with a builder when we married and then in 1966, he went to work on the docks, following in his father's footsteps. In October of that year my son Simon was born at home at Elsenham Road. We had brought the bed down into the front room, so I was on hand for the midwife. I still remember her having my afterbirth on a piece of newspaper and getting Bill to look at it! We stayed in that house for seven years.

We then moved to Humberston. Simon started school there and Michelle went into the juniors. Bill needed our car for work so if I wanted to go into town to my parents I had to go on the bus. I hated standing in the cold of winter at the bus stop with two children. We stayed in Humberston for around eighteen months and then moved to Louth Road. For a while I worked part time at the local grocery shop down Louth Road.

Our house was a nice bungalow with a big garden. It had fruit trees, so I used to bake pies. I put on quite a lot of weight living there. There was a small ornamental well in the front garden One day when I was a bit late home Simon decided to knock it down. That was another home that Bill altered. He knocked through a wall to make a kitchen/diner. He had a part-time job driving coaches while we lived there, which he enjoyed.

When Bill's father became ill, we moved back into town on Gilbey Road. Again, not that far from either of our parents. When we lived there lots of traffic went two ways and over Cleveland Bridge to the various factories. It seemed very noisy with all the cars going past on their way to work on the Humber Bank after living in Humberston, but I soon got used to it. That road is different now, with traffic only going one way. One Bonfire Night we had a bonfire in the garden. It got a little too high and nearly melted the telephone wires. The children enjoyed it, but I must say I was worried.

We moved into a newly built bungalow on Wybers Way. From there Michelle and Simon went to Whitgift school. Bill decided the bungalow wasn't big enough, so he made it into a house. Bill carried on part-time driving and I don't think either of us was happy. In April 1984 he said he had met someone else and was leaving me. At that time all I could think of was, how will I manage without a car?

A Special Person

Over the years my mother has been one of the most important people in my life. She was not very tall and rather plump. She had a round, happy face that had lots of wrinkles like an unironed shirt. She often wore a pinny that wrapped around her to cover her dress. In later years she always wore trousers. She was very outgoing and generous. As a child I went to Sunday School, but I was never forced to go. She was one of six children, and they were made to go twice each Sunday. I think her parents must have wanted a rest from childcare.

She had several jobs over the years, often cleaning at people's houses. I remember her mentioning cleaning for Mrs Rollett, mother of McKay & Rollett's optician. When I was young, she worked at the corner shop at the end of our cul-de-sac. It sold almost everything as shops in those days did.

She had a variety of hobbies and clearly wanted to better herself. I remember that at home she always had the radio on. One of her hobbies was reading. She loved Mills and Boon romantic stories, and in later years' biographies and non-fiction. She also loved writing and you will later see her words about my grandad. I think they were probably written when she was learning typing. She must have wanted to educate herself as she took night classes in shorthand and typing. She passed the exams and was accepted into the Civil Service, where she worked in work and pensions.

When she worked there, she became very interested in quizzes. She joined a team of her workmates and they played in the

Grimsby Quiz league with the team name of the Socialites and one year won a shield, which I still have. Often, she would be sat in her chair poring over an encyclopaedia. That is probably where I get my love of a quiz from, and my husband and I took her to pub quizzes with us which she enjoyed.

The following words were written by my mother about her father, my Grandad Tom, whom I never met, as he died earlier in the year before I was two years old, in August 1948. They are unchanged from how they were written more than fifty years ago.

Through my window mist hangs like a grey shroud over the fields and the gulls wing low in their endless search for food. When I hear the harsh screaming mew of the gulls I remember my father, for he was wont to say, "That's the loneliest sound on God's earth, lass." The seagulls' cry was an intrinsic part of his life. He was a fisherman. Three weeks at sea; then forty-eight hours ashore, before returning to pursue those elusive shoals of fish. And yet, despite the loneliness, the bitter conditions, through it all he retained the simplicity of a child in all things "bright and beautiful". He had the roll of a seaman when he walked, his face brown with the "salt water" weather, the deeply lined eyes of a man who is forever looking beyond the horizon. Although his hands were short and square with tufts of black hair below each knuckle, his hands could have graced the hands of a lady. They were a beautiful shape, oddly effeminate in such a rock of a man. Round his wrists were several salt-water boil scars, a legacy of wet clothes chafing the skin. When my mam put on a steaming hot linseed poultice, he never turned a hair. My mam and dad were very much in love, we rarely heard them quarrel. They had a special look for each other which excluded everyone else in the room. Even I, as a child, recognised it, though I had to grow up before I could put a name to it. All his life, to my mam, Dad was "Mate", she seldom called him by his baptismal name of Tom.

Being a fisherman, my father was naturally superstitious and Mam equally so. There were numerous taboos which we were honour bound to observe. For instance, we didn't walk in through the front door and out of the back door without first sitting down, as this was likely to take the luck out of the house. We didn't swing on any of the doors for the same reason. Saying the word PIG was regarded as sacrilege and we referred to those unfortunate animals as "grunters". Before disposing of our empty eggshells, we always punched a hole in the bottom, as there were witches ready to take the whole eggshell and sail in these frail craft to sink some unwary trawler. Mam would not wash clothes on the day my father sailed, not even if we hadn't a stitch to our backs, as you see she might unwittingly "wash him away". Someone once, optimistically, gave my dad a lucky black cat, but after a few bad trips when the fish were particularly evasive, he discovered it had green eyes. That presaged the mascot's death knell and into the dustbin it went. So too did Mam's best vase shortly after; its failing, like the cat's eyes, was its colour green. Green, to my father, was like a red rag to a bull. A fisherman couldn't do with anything around which invited unnecessary ill omen. Visitors to our house were always welcomed with the inevitable pot of tea, unless of course they happened to be new mothers who had failed to get themselves "churched". This is what we call the beautiful service in which a woman thanks God for the safe delivery of her child. Of course, I'm not superstitious now, "touch wood"!

Money was forever a problem to the parents of six growing children. There was a permanent absence of luxuries, but I remember vividly, when I was about eight years old, that Mam reached as near rock bottom as anyone possibly could. Dad broke his collar bone at sea during a particularly heavy storm and because there was no immediate medical aid, it didn't heal properly. Consequently, it was almost a year before he got back to sea. Because, as a ship's mate he didn't pay a "Lloyd George stamp" so he wasn't entitled to benefit (what we now call National Health). Too proud to go "on the parish", practically everything we owned was subsequently pawned. One incident I remember until the day I die. I discovered my mother crying bitterly because her wedding ring had to be pawned. Her bare finger was mute testimony to the dire straits into which we had fallen. "It's never been off my finger since the day your father put it there," she sobbed, broken-hearted. But God was good. Once redeemed it stayed on her finger. Today it is still her most precious possession. Moments of sorrow as deep as these were happily rare.

My father was born with a caul over his head and, because of it, a belief that he would never drown. He was proved right and died in his own bed with his family around him. I doubt if there will be another fisherman in our family, for the man who pursues those elusive shoals of fish must have salt water in his veins. He must have a strong faith to endure the rigours and the hardships. My father was such a man. I am proud to have known him for I shall never meet his like again.

About the Author

Rosanna McGlone is a writer, editor and arts consultant who runs a wide variety of community projects. She loves telling people's stories and supporting others to tell their tales.

Rosanna can be commissioned to work with community, heritage and arts organisations as the lead writer and to provide advice on longer creative projects, as well as to work with individuals on their memoirs. Having spent many years as a journalist, writing for, amongst others: the *Guardian*, the *Independent*, the *Weekend Australian* and the *Sydney Morning Herald,* Rosanna has a particular interest in non-fiction and biography. She also runs writing courses including Poetry Appreciation, Creative Writing and Memoir.

As a published author herself, Rosanna has had a diverse career. Her work has been supported by Old Vic, New Voices and Arts Council England and been performed at Vault Festival and Hull Truck Theatre where she was invited to become a reader. Her first radio play reached the final 20 in the BBC's Alfred Bradley Bursary Award. Rosanna is a member of the Society of Authors and her latest piece of short fiction will be published by Muswell Press in 2021.

If you would like to hear our stories in person, work with Rosanna on a project of your own or buy this book, please email mcglonehealey@gmail.com, or telephone 07570 480802.

Acknowledgements

Sincere thanks to the Care Plus Group Charitable Trust for commissioning this project. I am also grateful to Toni Herron from Friendship at Home for her support with *My Mother's Purse*; Sarah Taylor-Fergusson for her eagle eye in proofreading this anthology; Jamie from Imprint Digital for his advice regarding its printing and to Alan Birchall for doing everything which no one else could do.

RHINE ARMY SUMMER

To Jimmy Reid —
who knows where all the
bodies are buried
with regards
Colin [illegible]
Exeter 2008